D1565928

ARMED *with* FAITH

The life of

Father Vincent R. Capodanno, MM

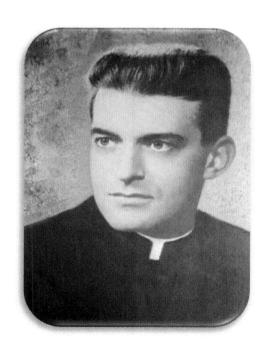

Stephen M. DiGiovanni

Prepared by the Historical Commission of the Cause for Canonization
for Father Vincent R. Capodanno, MM,
The Most Reverend Timothy P. Broglio, J.C.D.,
Archdiocese for Military Services, USA.

Historical Commission of the Cause for Canonization:
Reverend Monsignor Stephen M. DiGiovanni
Reverend Monsignor Robert F. Trisco
Reverend Daniel L. Mode

For Father Capodanno's family;
their inspiration made a Saint

"Chaplain (Lt.) Vincent R. Capodanno, 37,

of New York City [sic],

wears no physical weapon of war.

HIS ARMAMENT is faith –

a basic, necessary and treasured attribute

to the men around him."

"Chaplain, Ex-Taiwan Missionary
Feels His Job is With Viet Troops,"
The American Weekend (The Marine Corps Press),
October 19, 1966

Table of Contents

Archival Sources and Abbreviations 1

Foreword by Archbishop Broglio 3

Chapter I: Vincent Robert 7

Chapter II: Formosa and Language School 29

Chapter III: The Missions in Tunglo and Miaoli 45

Chapter IV: Hong Kong and Hawaii 73

Chapter V: Training and Vietnam, 1966 103

Chapter VI: Vietnam, 1967 135

Chapter VII: September 4, 1967 149

Epilogue 165

Appendix I: Mission Diaries, 1958-1959 169

Appendix II:
Some Reflections on Adaptation to the Orient,
Father Vincent R. Capodanno, MM, November 1966................. 199

Biographical Timeline of Father Vincent R. Capodanno, MM,
1929-1967 205

Bibliography 215

Archival Sources and Abbreviations

ACUA: The American Catholic History Research Center and University Archives, The Catholic University of America, Washington, D.C.

AMIL: Archives of the Archdiocese for Military Services, USA, Washington, D.C.

CAP/Staten: Capodanno Family papers, Staten Island, NY.

MFBA: Maryknoll Mission Archives, Ossining, NY.

NAV/Cap: Naval Chaplaincy School Archives, Fort Jackson, SC.

N.d.:   No date of composition indicated in a document.

N.p.:   No place of origin indicated in a document.

Foreword

As I sit on a terrace overlooking Santiago de Compostela, I can see many pilgrims and tourists crowded on the streets. Walking the Camino has become even more popular as pilgrims from around the world walk toward their goal: the tomb of the Apostle James.

We make pilgrimages for many reasons, but fundamentally we are reminded that life is a pilgrimage and the goal is life eternal, that is to dwell in the presence of Almighty God. Throughout the pilgrimage of life we are encouraged by many people. Parents, catechists, priests, and the example of holy men and women whose lives indicated a closeness to the Lord.

Those mentors teach us how to walk on the road of life. They inspire us to soar above the mediocre or the lowest common denominator. Their lives tell us that the goal is possible. We can go forward. We can grow in holiness, courage, and Christ-like fidelity.

In the pages that follow, an excellent writer and historian, Monsignor Stephen M. DiGiovanni, introduces the reader to the figure of the Servant of God, Father Vincent R. Capodanno, priest, missionary, and chaplain to the United States Marine Corps.

Several years ago I asked Msgr. DiGiovanni to serve as the chairman of the Historical Commission in the Cause for the recognition of the sanctity of this hero. He carefully studied the documentation available and spoke to those who knew Father Capodanno during his life. This book offers the results of that study and is being published to help others learn about the priest who gave his life to minister to "his Marines."

While you will certainly appreciate the careful research and the literary talents of the pastor of the Basilica of Saint John the Evangelist in Stamford, CT, my hope is that you are also captured by the virtues of the pilgrim whose example has inspired so many.

Father Capodanno was an average student who worked during the summers of seminary college years to pay for his education and support his family. His local Maryknoll Superiors did not always favor his growth as a priest and missionary. In fact, his unexpected and undesired transfer to Hong Kong in 1965 set the stage for his association with sailors and marines and his decision to request permission to serve as a Navy chaplain.

Those ordinary traits, struggles, disappointments, and continued fidelity help all of us who still walk our pilgrimage with hopes, dreams, and reverses.

Therefore, continuing the work begun by my predecessor, Edwin Cardinal O'Brien, I have encouraged the work on the Cause and established the Capodanno Guild, because I believe that the heroism and commitment of this Servant of God can help all of us on our pilgrimage. We need good examples. We can profit from the lives of seemingly ordinary people who respond in extraordinary ways to the situations that make up their lives.

I may be able to watch pilgrims for a time, but then I must return to my own segment of the journey. It is good to be able to do so with the example of others whose lives tell me that the goal is within my grasp. It is only necessary to draw on the gifts received and to keep moving forward.

Msgr. DiGiovanni, please accept my gratitude for your earnest efforts and for the honor of penning the lines of this Foreword. You continue to be an inspiration to many and I am glad that you are offering this book for the encouragement of all pilgrims on the road to life without end.

+ Timothy P. Broglio

Archbishop for the Military Services, USA

July 11, 2018
Feast of Saint Benedict, Patron of Europe

ARMED *with* FAITH

Chapter I

Vincent Robert

Vincent Robert Capodanno, Sr. was a native of Gaeta, Italy, who emigrated to the United States in 1901. He found work in New York City as a ship's caulker.[1] His future wife, Rachel Basile, whose family was from Sorrento, Italy, was born in the United States. They were married in the Brooklyn Church of the Sacred Hearts of Jesus and Mary on December 15, 1907.[2] Vincent was 22; Rachel, 18. In 1908, the family moved to Mariners Harbor, Staten Island, New York, and opened a small vegetable store.[3]

Vincent Robert, Jr. was born on February 13, 1929 in the family home, 105 Winant Street, Staten Island, New York. The youngest of ten children, he was named after his father, Vincent Robert, and known to friends and family as "Junior."[4] He was baptized on April 28, 1929 by Father E.E. Molinelli in the Church of Saint Michael, Mariners Harbor, Staten Island. He later received his First Holy Communion and Confirmation on April 21, 1937 at the nearby Church of Saint Clement.[5]

His was a happy home life, growing up in a large family. The first unhappiness of his life occurred as he approached his tenth birthday: he was struck by a car, leaving him with a broken arm. Then, on his tenth birthday, February 13, 1939, his father,

---

[1] MFBA, Box: Capodanno Personnel Files; Folder: Capodanno, Rev. Vincent R/Documents: Certificates.

[2] MFBA, Box: Capodanno Personnel Files; Folder: Capodanno, Rev. Vincent R/Documents. Marriage Certificate.

[3] Mode, Daniel L., *The Grunt Padre* (Oak Lawn, Ill, 2000), p. 5.

[4] MFBA, Box: Capodanno Personnel Files; Folder: Capodanno, Rev. Vincent R/Documents. "State of New York Certificate and Record of Birth." AMIL, Box: Capodanno *Mementoes* 1. P. S. 44 Graduation Remembrance Book. January 19, 1943: "Dearest Cousin Junior: May your life be filled with everlasting joys and happiness! Your loving cousin, Jeannette."

[5] Parish of St. Clement and St. Michael, Staten Island: Sacramental Records.

Vincent Sr., died of a cerebral hemorrhage while working on a barge in the Hudson River. He was 53 years old. The family united around their mother, even as the older children began leaving home to begin their adult lives.

Young Vincent received his grammar school education at the local public school, P.S. 44 at 44 Maple Parkway on Staten Island. His school work was consistently reported as "satisfactory" [the only other report card category was "unsatisfactory"] with repeated teacher recommendations that he work to improve his penmanship, spelling and, later, arithmetic. His strongest subjects were reading, literature, geography and history.[6] By September 1940, Vincent stood nearly 5 feet tall [59 inches], weighed 91 pounds, and was a healthy, active boy.[7] His classmates voted Vincent "The Best Looking" and "The Best Dresser" among the male student graduates of 1943. He kept a small graduation remembrance book that includes the names of his teachers, autographs by his friends, photographs, and student lists. He recorded his favorite people and things, as well as his ideas for his future education and professional career as a medical doctor:

> Favorite Author: Howard Pease [8]
>
> Favorite Book: "All of them"
>
> Favorite Song: *Star Spangled Banner*
>
> Favorite Sport: Swimming
>
> Favorite Hero: General MacArthur

---

[6] AMIL, Box: Childhood Album. Board of Education City of New York, 1938-1940 P.S. 44 Report Cards.

[7] AMIL, Box: Childhood Album. Board of Education City of New York, 1940-1941 P.S. 44 Report Card.

[8] Howard Pease (1894–1974) was "an American writer of adventure stories from Stockton, California. Most of his stories revolved around a young protagonist, Joseph Todhunter ('Tod') Moran, who shipped out on tramp freighters during the interwar years" [Wikipedia].

Favorite Chum: Philip Tenerielo

High School: Curtis High

Profession: "M.D." [Medical Doctor]

Motto: "Do a good turn daily."

On one of the first pages of this small, leather bound remembrance book, dated January 18, 1943, Vincent composed a brief poem:

So, little album, far and near,

to all my friends I hold so dear,

and ask them each to write a page

that I may read in my old age.

Vincent Capodanno.[9]

Vincent graduated from the eighth grade in January, 1943, and enrolled in the local public Curtis High School as a freshman of the graduating class of 1947. Throughout his high school years his grades remained average; consistently high in Latin and History, consistently unimpressive in English Grammar and Elementary Science.[10] He was a member of the Biology Honor Society, was elected a class officer, and was a counselor for the Catholic Youth Organization (CYO) at his home parish of Our Lady of Good Counsel.[11]

Vincent graduated from high school on February 4, 1947, ranked 53rd among the 149 graduating students. In order to help his widowed mother with the household expenses, he began work as a clerk in the Pearl Insurance Company at 19 Rector Street, in New York City. In 1948, he also began attending night classes at the downtown Manhattan campus of Fordham

---

[9] AMIL, Box: Childhood & Seminary Binder. P.S. 44 Graduation Remembrance Book.

[10] AMIL, Ibid, Childhood Album. Curtis High School Report Cards: 1943-1947.

[11] Mode, Daniel L., *The Grunt Padre* (Oak Lawn, Il, 2000), p. 12.

University.[12] During this period, Vincent frequently met a classmate from Curtis High School, William Richter, since both attended daily morning Mass at Our Lady of Victory Church and traveled to work on the Staten Island Ferry. They frequently attended Exposition and Benediction of the Most Blessed Sacrament at their home parish in the evenings. In the spring of 1949, both young men made a retreat, during which Vincent revealed his thoughts about studying for the priesthood. Vincent believed his friend was called to the priesthood as well, but William dismissed the notion. Years later, however, he admitted that Vincent ". . . did plant the idea and, after some discernment . . . I decided to enter the Maryknoll seminary."[13]

By mid-summer 1949, Vincent seriously considered applying to the Catholic Foreign Mission Society of America, commonly known as Maryknoll. He discussed his possible priestly vocation with some priests in his home parish and at Fordham.[14] Despite not personally knowing any Maryknoll priest well, he admitted on his application that he had been thinking specifically about Maryknoll "for about six months" prior to applying. Vincent wrote on his application to Maryknoll, "I wanted to go into the priesthood and the idea of serving in the mission was strongest in my mind."[15]

The Catholic Foreign Mission Society of America was founded by two diocesan priests: Fathers James A. Walsh of Boston, Massachusetts, and Thomas F. Price of Raleigh, North Carolina. The Society was approved during the annual meeting

---

[12]MFBA, Box: Capodanno Personnel Files. Father Capodanno's academic transcripts, dated August 30, 1965, were provided by Maryknoll to the Military Ordinariate upon Vincent's application to become a military chaplain.

[13] Mode, *The Grunt Padre*, p. 13.

[14] MFBA, Box: Capodanno Personnel Files; Folder: Capodanno, Rev. Vincent R/Documents. N.p. , May 15, 1947, Memorandum, Rev. Walter L. Mackesy, MM; Staten Island May 1, 1949, Rev. James H. Griffen, O.S.A. to "Dear Father."

[15] MFBA, Box: Capodanno Personnel Files, Folder: Capodanno, Rev. Vincent R/Documents. "Application for Admittance as a Maryknoll Student," p. 2.

of the American Archbishops in Washington, D.C. on April 27, 1911, and authorized by Pope Saint Pius X on June 29, 1911. The general purpose of Maryknoll was to place its American resources and manpower at the disposal of the Holy See by responding to the needs of the Congregation of the Propaganda Fide in establishing the Church in mission territories outside the United States.

Writing of the missionary spirit then developing in the United States, Bishop John M. Merel, one of the early Vicars Apostolic of Canton, China, wrote that the Church in the United States had matured, signs of which were the establishment of the hierarchy, two American dioceses raised to the dignity of cardinalatial sees, and the development of prosperous religious orders. He continued, "She was famous among the Churches of the world, but her greatness was not complete yet; she had no shelter for the young priests who aspired to go and preach to the heathen in the field afar."[16]

Vincent Capodanno was one such aspiring young man. He first learned of Maryknoll by reading the mission magazine, *The Field Afar*, the first issue of which appeared in January, 1907. Vincent was inspired by the mission stories he read, as he explained in his application:

> I first heard of the Maryknolls (sic) through "Field Afar" [sic]. I admired them for it but never thought too much about it. When I decided to go into the foreign mission field I remembered all I had read about the Maryknolls [sic] and decided that was what I wanted to do. [17]

Likewise, he described his idea of the life and work of a missioner, in response to a question on the application form:

---

[16] Quoted in Powers, George C., *The Maryknoll Movement* (Maryknoll, NY, 1926), p. 55.

[17] MFBA, Box: Capodanno Personnel Files; Folder: Capodanno, Rev. Vincent R/Documents, "Application for Admittance as a Maryknoll Student," p. 4.

It will mean hard physical labor with and for a group of people I may never have even heard of before. I'll be separated from my family and friends, and all the things I'm now accustomed to for indefinite lengths of time, during which all my efforts will be devoted to the people I'm serving. Their lives, both troubles and joys will be my life. Any personal sacrifice I may have to make will be compensated for by the fact that I'm serving God.[18]

Those asked by Vincent to provide letters of recommendation wrote that he was a good young man, capable in his studies, and a suitable candidate for Maryknoll. Father John J. Hooper, SJ, an assistant dean of Fordham University, wrote:

He seems to be a quiet, refined young man. His general averages run in B's, and I know that for some time he has been interested in entering Maryknoll. Further than that I cannot actually go, because it is quite difficult to get to know most evening students well.[19]

Mr. John Avent, principal of Curtis High School, wrote:

Vincent graduated from Curtis [High School] in February 1947. As his record will show, he maintained a good average in most subjects and did a particularly good piece of work on his Latin 3 Years. He was recommended by all his teachers as a cooperative and likable student. We believe that he will be an acceptable member of a college group.[20]

---

[18] MFBA, MFBA, Box: Capodanno Personnel Files, Folder: Capodanno, Rev. Vincent R/Documents. "Application for Admittance as a Maryknoll Student," p. 4.

[19] MFBA, Box: Capodanno Personnel Files; Folder: Capodanno, Rev. Vincent R/Documents. NYC, March 23, 1949, Rev. John J. Hooper, SJ to Father James P. Courneen, MM

[20] MFBA, Box: Capodanno Personnel Files. Folder: Capodanno, Rev. Vincent R/Documents. Staten Island, March 30, 1949, John M. Avent to Father James Courneen, MM

Father James H. Griffin, OSA, pastor of Our Lady of Good Counsel Parish, wrote:

> Vincent Capodanno of 259 Castleton Avenue, is a member of this parish. He is of good moral character and is worthy of consideration.[21]

His family was surprised by Vincent's decision to become a priest and a Maryknoll missioner. The family had expected Vincent's elder brother, Albert Capodanno, to enter the seminary. Vincent was to become a medical doctor. Vincent's mother had reservations as well. As James Capodanno remembered, "She found it difficult because Vince was the youngest son." [22] So serious, that Father Walter L. Mackesy, MM, visited the Capodanno home in May, 1949 to discuss the matter with Mrs. Capodanno. Father Mackesy briefly described his visit in a private memorandum:

> Vicnet [sic] is one of Father Courneen's lads from first year Fordahm [sic] College. [I] Dropped in on him the other day while in Staten Island to iron things out with his mother. Father deceased, and Vin is the youngest of six or seven kiddos. Mother feels that he's being a bit selfish to leave her, etc., but finally came around to our way of thinking. He's third generation in this country. Nice home, nice family and mother won't stand in his way. Not a lack of faith, just expecting the worse [sic]. Vin looks OK. Should do well as a missioner.[23]

Father James P. Courneen, MM, had studied at Fordham College. He later recalled that, while in his third year studying business

---

[21] MFBA, Box: Capodanno Personnel Files. Folder: Capodanno, Rev. Vincent R/Documents. Staten Island, May 1, 1949, Father James H. Griffin, OSA to "Dear Father."

[22] MAMIL, Box: Capodanno Personal Testimonies. Staten Island, January 6, 2014, Interview by the author of James Capodanno.

[23] MFBA, Box: Capodanno Personnel Files. Folder: Capodanno, Rev. Vincent R/Documents. N.p., n.d., Memorandum, Father Walter L. Mackesy, MM. Note on top right corner: "Received May 16, 1949."

administration, he decided to enter Maryknoll, which he did in 1940, and was ordained a priest in 1945. For the subsequent ten years, both he and Father Walter L. Mackesy, MM, were involved in development work for Maryknoll, seeking contributions and seminarians for the mission society. While students at Fordham, the young James Courneen and the younger Vincent Capodanno were both captivated by the same Maryknoll magazine, *The Field Afar*. It is quite plausible that as Vincent was considering a priestly vocation while studying at Fordham, he spoke with Father Courneen, the ever friendly, voluble, very persuasive and dedicated Maryknoll missionary priest.[24]

As Vincent considered the priesthood and Maryknoll, world events underscored the need for dedicated Catholic priests and laity in the face of the aggressive threat of atheistic Communism in Europe and Asia. Following the sentencing of Cardinal Jozsef Mindszenty of Hungary by the Communist government on February 8, 1949, Monsignor Fulton J. Sheen urged Catholics to be strong. He particularly encouraged Catholics in China to prepare to suffer for their Catholic faith:

> The coming struggle is not a contest between Communism and Fascism, because they are not two diametrically opposed things, but the struggle will be between a society which believes in God and a society which makes itself God. Therefore one cannot say a few words about atheism and Communism being enemies of the people and then pat oneself on the back and think he has fulfilled his duty as a Christian. God did not send us into the world to declaim against evil, but to correct evil; he did not send us to cry out 'unclean', but to purify uncleanliness; He did not send us to judge but to save. Our duty is not only to testify against our neighbor's errors or to prove our own orthodoxy, but our God-given

---

[24] Maryknoll, February 12, 2014, Father Michael Walsh, MM, to Monsignor Stephen M. DiGiovanni. Father Walsh is the archivist of the Maryknoll Mission Archives in Ossining, NY.

responsibility is to teach Christ, the Crucified Christ, in order that Truth will win over all.[25]

Maryknoll had a strong presence in China, both on the mainland and on Formosa, today's Taiwan. As Vincent began his seminary studies, the first native born Chinese bishop was consecrated on October 7, 1949: Ignatius Kung Pin-Mei, the founding bishop of Soochow, China. He was consecrated by Archbishop Anthony Riberi, the Apostolic Internuncio, soon to be exiled from China, assisted by Bishop Simon Tsu of Haimen and by Bishop James E. Walsh, MM, a Maryknoll missioner, who was later arrested and imprisoned by the Communists with Bishop Kung in 1955.[26] These were impressive examples of heroic dedication and self-sacrifice for a young man considering priestly service in the foreign missions in Asia. During Vincent's college and major seminary years of study, the Communist onslaught against the Catholic Church intensified, especially in Korea and China.

By May, 1949, Vincent was notified by mail that he was accepted into the college seminary program of Maryknoll. He was assigned to begin a summer course in Latin, from June 25th until August 3rd, 1949, at Maryknoll's high school preparatory seminary—The Venard—in Clarks Summit, Pennsylvania. Because Vincent studied in public schools, he was told summer classes in Latin were judged necessary ". . . since you will be slightly behind your own class in this subject."[27]

The seminary annual tuition was $425.00. Those studying at The Venard were expected to pay $250.00, the balance to be secured by benefactors, if possible. Vincent responded to the question on the seminary application concerning his method of

---

[25] *China Missionary*, Vol. II, April 1949, No. 4, p. 430.

[26] *China Missionary Bulletin*, Vol. II (III), January 1950, No. 1, p. 95.

[27] MFBA, Box: Capodanno Personnel Files. Folder: Capodanno, Rev. Vincent R/Documents. Maryknoll, May 18, 1949, Rev. James Smith, MM, to Vincent Capodanno [copy].

payment for the balance of the tuition: "Over the summer months I'll be able to save $200.00. From then on just the money I'll be able to make in my own free time."[28] Vincent's summer was filled with the study of classical prose, in which he scored a 77 out of a possible 100 for his final grade. [29]

Following his summer Latin studies, Vincent was informed by the newly-appointed rector of the Maryknoll college seminary in Glen Ellyn, Illinois, that his studies there would not begin until late October, because of construction. The rector suggested that ". . . if you can get a job for the summer it would be well to work as long as possible into September," a suggestion that proved helpful for Vincent struggling to pay his own college seminary tuition. [30] During the remaining summer weeks at home, Vincent returned to the Pearl Insurance Company in New York City.

Vincent's freshman academic year of 1949-1950 at the Maryknoll College in Glen Ellyn, Illinois, was uneventful. The summer weeks at The Venard had given Vincent some idea of his seminary years at the larger Maryknoll college seminary, which housed 300 seminarians. His academic work consisted primarily of introductory courses: The Life of Christ: The Mass; Freshman Classical Latin II; Composition I; Modern European History I; Elementary French; General Introduction to Chemistry, and Music Theory I. His worst course during the first semester was Music Theory, with a grade of 60. His first semester academic average was 77.00, ranked 48 of 85 students. His second semester academic grade average was 80.52, and he ranked 39

---

[28] MFBA, Box: Capodanno Personnel Files. Folder: Capodanno, Rev. Vincent R/Documents, "Application for Admittance as a Maryknoll Student," p. 6.

[29] MFBA, Box: Capodanno, Personnel File. Folder: Capodanno, Rev. Vincent R/Documents, Glen Ellyn, Il, August 30, 1965, Maryknoll Seminary, College Department, Academic Transcript.

[30] MFBA, Box: Capodanno, Personnel Files. Folder: Capodanno, Rev. Vincent R/Documents, Clarks Summit, PA, August 19, 1949, Father Arthur C. Kiernan, MM, to Vincent R. Capodanno.

of 84 students, giving him a general average for the year of 78.760. He improved in Music Theory during the second semester, with a final grade of 85.[31]

Father James R. Jackson, MM, later recalled his experience as Vincent's roommate at Glen Ellyn. He commented on Vincent's cleanliness, obviously the fruit of his training at home. After the death of his father, when Vincent was still a boy, the family home was directed by his mother and his five older sisters. The sisters set the tone, assigned the chores and trained the boys in all aspects of personal hygiene and cleanliness, which formation served the brothers throughout their lives. Father Jackson recalled,

> I have heard it said that cleanliness is near to holiness. If that is true, then Vince should have been canonized a long time ago. He insisted that we mop the floor every morning, (even under the bed) and clean the sink every time we used it. It was important to dry the sink as well, seeing as dust accumulated more on a wet surface. If Vince had any influence on my life it was this: till this day I continue to wash the sink after using it, although I don't dry it. It was mystifying to me how he could keep his cassock and black suit free of lint. That was the most orderly and sanitary five months of my entire life. [32]

Vincent was active in sports; his favorite was hand ball. Father Jackson remembered that Vincent had an easy way about him, getting along well with the other students. During the summer vacation, he visited Vincent at his sister's home in Arlington, New Jersey. A neighbor had a pool, and they enjoyed swimming during the hot summer days, and discussed books they were reading during the vacation. "Vince was a humble guy,

---

[31] MFBA, Box: Capodanno, Personnel Files. Folder: Capodanno, Rev. Vincent R/Documents, Glen Ellyn, IL, August 30, 1965, Maryknoll Seminary, College Department, Academic Transcript.

[32] AMIL, Box: Capodanno Personal Testimonies. Shiga-ken, Japan, May 10, 2007, Father James R. Jackson, MM, to Mary Preece, 1r.

which made it easy to hold long, laid-back conversations. I always remember him as a person who put people at ease. And I must add that he also had a sense of humor."[33]

His sophomore year, 1950-1951, was spent at the Maryknoll Junior College in Lakewood, New Jersey, where he studied Moral Theology; English Literature; Patristic and Medieval Latin; Composition; French; Fundamentals of Public Speaking; Modern European History; and his least favorite subject, Music. His general grade average for the academic year was lower: 72.857, with a final ranking of 50 among 65 students.[34]

It was during this academic year that the reality of priestly missionary work was brought closer to home, when two Maryknoll bishops were arrested by the communists in Korea and China. Bishop Patrick J. Byrne, MM, one of the first students to enter Maryknoll, who, after ten years of service at Maryknoll, was assigned to Korea in 1923. Bishop Francis Xavier Ford, MM, was one of the first Maryknoll missionaries assigned to China in 1918. Following the outbreak of hostilities in Korea in 1950, Bishop Byrne was arrested along with other priests, religious sisters and laity. In November 1950, he died of pneumonia while in captivity. Bishop Ford was arrested in Canton, China in December, 1950, dying two years later after enduring torture, maltreatment and starvation in prison.

The militant reality of Chinese Communism was no longer something distant, the experience of which was limited to newspapers. It was made very real by the martyrdom of these two of Maryknoll's greatest missioners, whose ranks young Vincent Capodanno would soon join. The memory and examples of these heroic Maryknoll missionaries could hardly be

---

[33] AMIL, Ibid.

[34] MFBA, Box: Capodanno, Personnel Files. Folder: Capodanno, Rev. Vincent R/Documents, Glen Ellyn, IL, August 30, 1965, Maryknoll Seminary, College Department, Academic Transcript.

forgotten, especially by those sent to the mission fields of the Far East.

During his final two years of college seminary, Vincent's final grade average for his junior year, 1951-1952, was 79.178, with a ranking of 67 among 90 students; for his senior year, 1952-1953, he attained a final average of 81.370, graduating with a ranking of 43 among 80 students, and a general average for the four years of 80.188.[35]

Upon the completion of his seminary undergraduate studies in philosophy in June, 1953, Vincent returned to his family home for the summer months. He also returned to the Pearl Insurance Company in New York City, in order to continue helping his mother and to pay his college tuition. He assisted at daily Mass at Our Lady of Good Counsel Parish and attended evening devotions at Our Lady of Mount Carmel Church near his family home.[36]

Vincent entered the Maryknoll novitiate in Bedford, Massachusetts after the summer vacation. There he continued his spiritual and academic preparation for major seminary and Maryknoll life throughout the 1953/1954 academic year. He studied Ascetical Theology, Liturgy and Catechetics.[37] Upon completion of his novitiate year, on August 30, 1954, Vincent took his first solemn oath, publicly stating his free choice to continue his preparation for the priesthood in the Catholic Foreign Mission Society of America.[38]

Vincent then began his major seminary studies at The Knoll, the home of Maryknoll in the Society's mother house in

---

[35] MFBA, Box: Capodanno, Personnel Files. Folder: Capodanno, Rev. Vincent R/Documents, Maryknoll Seminary, College Department, Office of the Registrar.

[36] Mode, *The Grunt Padre,* p. 28.

[37] MFBA, Box: Capodanno Personnel Files. Folder: Capodanno, Rev. Vincent R/Documents: Maryknoll Seminary Scholastic Record.

[38] MFBA, Box: Capodanno Personnel Files. Folder: Capodanno, Rev. Vincent R/Documents: Personnel File Card.

Ossining, New York. The building is of rough local stone, with Roman arches and Oriental architectural elements. Begun in 1920, construction was still in progress when Vincent arrived in the late summer of 1954, and continued through 1956. Vincent received Tonsure on September 17, 1954.

A fellow Maryknoller, Father Thomas Donnelly, MM, lived and studied with Father Vincent while they were both at The Knoll. Father Donnelly was one ordination class ahead of Father Capodanno. "He [Vincent] was quiet, did his manual labor and morning duties jobs in the seminary very well. At one point I was the overseer for such jobs."[39] Father Donnelly further recalled that Vincent Capodanno participated in all intramural sports at the seminary, including touch football, basketball, softball, soccer, swimming and tennis.

By May, 1955, Vincent and his 57 classmates were promoted to their second year of theological studies, and "approved for promotion to First Minor Orders and their next Temporary Oath."[40] He received Porter and Lector on June 9, 1955; took his second oath on September 15, 1955; received Exorcist and Acolyte on June 7, 1956; and took his third and final temporary oath on September 13, 1956.[41] The decision to persevere in his priestly vocation was obviously strong, and he began using the little funds he had to purchase the necessities of the priesthood, such as a set of breviaries. He wrote to his sister Pauline, informing her that as a Christmas savings account [Christmas Club] had matured, "I intend to use part of it to pay for my breviaries. Come next June when I begin to say the Divine Office, every day you can count on being

---

[39] AMIL, Box: Capodanno, Mode File, Kamuela, HI, July 7, 2001, Father Thomas Donnelly, MM, to Father Daniel L. Mode.

[40] MFBA, Box 6: Council Meetings Minutes 1949-54. Folder; General Council Minutes, 1954-55.

[41] MFBA, Box: Capodanno Personnel Files. Folder: Capodanno, Rev. Vincent R/Documents: Personnel File Card.

prayed for in my Office."[42] Vincent was approved by the General Council for advancement to Subdiaconate and the taking of the Perpetual Oath,[43] which he made on June 6, 1957.[44]

As his final summer prior to diaconate ordination began, Mrs. Capodanno suffered a fall, resulting in a broken hip that required extended hospitalization, draining the already meager family finances. Vincent wrote his Maryknoll superiors on June 26, 1957, explained the situation, and requested a $1,000.00 loan [$8,438.11 in 2016 dollars] from the Society.[45]

During the Maryknoll General Council meeting of October 1, it was decided to grant an interest-free loan to the young deacon. "The loan will be his responsibility and it will be up to him to make what arrangements he can with the other members of his family for its repayment. There will be no interest charge on the loan and it should be repaid within a year."[46]

Vincent was also granted a temporary leave of absence from the seminary residence to be with his mother to help in her recovery, during which time he spent hours at her bedside.[47]

By early November, Mrs. Capodanno returned home, as her son reported to his superiors:

> My mother is leaving the hospital today. She, I and

[42] AMIL, Box: Correspondence Binder. N.p., November 18, 1956, Vincent Capodanno to Pauline & George.

[43] MFBA, Box 7: General Council Meetings Minutes, 1955-1963. Folder: General Council Minutes, 1956-57.

[44] MFBA, Box: Capodanno Personnel Files. Folder: Capodanno, Rev. Vincent R/Documents: Personnel File Card.

[45] MFBA, Box: Capodanno Personnel Files. Folder: Capodanno, Rev. Vincent R/Documents. Note referring to the letter is found in the October 1, 1957 Memorandum, Father T.S. Walsh, MM, to Fr. Manning, MM. CPI Inflation Calculator: www.data.bls.gov/cgi-bin/cpicalc.pl

[46] MFBA, Box 7: Council Meetings Minutes, 1955-63. Folder: General Council Minutes: 1957-58, p. 21: Tuesday, October 1, 1957.

[47] Mode, *The Grunt Padre,* p. 32.

the whole family are confident that her progress has, in a great measure, been due to the prayers offered for her by my fellow Maryknollers.

She has asked me to thank everyone for their generous and kind prayerful rememberance [sic] of her while she was hospitalized and has assured me of her own prayers, past and yet to come, for all here.

It will be several weeks before she can get up on her feet and several months before she will be able to walk unaided. Therefore, while she sends her heartfelt thanks for the prayers already sent, she also requests that we all continue to keep her in our prayers.

I too want to extend my own thanks to the faculty as well as to my fellow seminarians for the thoughtfulness and charity they have shown by keeping my mother in their prayers.[48]

While attending to his mother during the summer, Vincent also worked at Mary Immaculate Hospital in Jamaica, New York.[49] He was ordained to the Diaconate on September 14, 1957.[50]

During the winter semester of Vincent's last seminary year, the seminary faculty and the Father General conducted final evaluations and formal interviews of each deacon as a final analysis of each candidate, and as a means to help determine each man's first mission assignment. In his "Visitation Report" of February, 1958, Father John W. Comber, MM, Superior General of Maryknoll, made these notes about his meeting with Deacon Vincent Capodanno:

---

[48] MFBA, Box: Capodanno Personnel Files. Folder: Capodanno, Rev. Vincent R/Documents. Maryknoll, November 7, 1957, Vincent R. Capodanno to Father Malone, MM.

[49] AMIL, Box: Funeral Binder. N.p., N.d. [1967], Mr. & Mrs. Luhmann to Mrs. Costa.

[50] MFBA, Box: Capodanno Personnel File. Folder: Capodanno, Rev. Vincent R/Documents: Maryknoll Seminary Scholastic Record.

He had a lot to say and said it in quite a belligerent manner. I do not think he meant to sound belligerent. He did not wish to speak about rules such as going to bed at 10 P.M. or no smoking after breakfast, but he wanted to speak about the philosophy of the system which doesn't let deacons decide some things for themselves, that no sense of responsibility is developed, etc., etc."[51]

This would not be the last time Vincent spoke honestly and candidly with his superiors, offering suggestions for changes in the Maryknoll rule that he felt outdated. He would do the same once in Taiwan, and continued to offer his suggestions to his Maryknoll superiors while he served in Vietnam, urging changes in the manner in which the work of the foreign missions was carried out.

On March 31, 1958, the Maryknoll General Council gave final approval to the mission assignments for those to be ordained priests, as well as for transfers of veteran Maryknoll missioners to new assignments. Assigned to the Formosa Region, which included Taichung and Miaoli on Formosa [Taiwan], and Hong Kong, were Fathers Cyril V. Hirst, Edward L. Kumplemann, John A. Carbin and Donald J. Sheehan; and Deacons Joseph A. Kimmerling, Raymond H. Kelley, and Vincent R. Capodanno. Deacon Capodanno and Father Sheehan were assigned to a one year language course on Formosa before beginning their actual mission assignment.[52] Two weeks later, the General Council approved Vincent and his 47 deacon classmates "for

---

[51] MFBA, Box: Capodanno Personnel File. Folder: Capodanno, Rev. Vincent R/Documents: Most Rev. John W. Comber, MM, "Visitation Report, Maryknoll, NY, February 1958."

[52] MFBA, Box 7: Council Meetings Minutes 1955-63. Folder: General Council Minutes 1957-58, "Council Minutes: July 1, 1957 to June 30, 1958," p. 74: Monday, March 31, 1958.

advancement to the Priesthood."[53]

Vincent was awarded both a Bachelor's Degree in Sacred Theology, and a Master's Degree in Moral Theology, on June 7, 1958.[54] His Master's dissertation was entitled, "The Morality of Non-directive Counseling."[55] This study would serve him well in Vietnam.

Vincent and his classmates were ordained to the priesthood on June 14, 1958 by Francis Cardinal Spellman, Archbishop of New York. Vincent's mother, siblings and friends attended the ordination.

On the following day, June 15th, Father Capodanno offered his first Low Mass for his family and friends prior to the official Departure Ceremony. As the Departure Bell rang out in The Knoll courtyard, Archbishop Thomas A. Boland of Newark, New Jersey and Father John W. Comber, MM, Superior General of Maryknoll, gave each man his mission cross and assignment. Father Capodanno's assignment read:

> By the authority of the Sacred Congregation of Propaganda Fide and the Constitutions of the Catholic Foreign Mission Society of America, you are hereby formally assigned to labor for souls in the Maryknoll Mission Region of Formosa.
>
> May God bless you and may our Mother Mary protect you.[56]

---

[53] MFBA, Box 7: Council Meetings Minutes 1955-63. Folder: General Council Minutes 1957-58, "Council Minutes: July 1, 1957 to June 30, 1958," p. 79: Tuesday, April 15, 1958.

[54] MFBA, Box: Capodanno Personnel File. Folder: Capodanno, Rev. Vincent R/Documents: Personnel File Card.

[55] MFBA, Box: Personnel Files. Folder: Capodanno, Rev. Vincent R/Documents. Maryknoll Seminary Scholastic Record.

[56] MFBA, Box: Capodanno Personnel Files. Folder: Capodanno, Rev. Vincent R/Documents. N.p., June 15, 1958, Father John W. Comber, MM, to Father Vincent R. Capodanno, MM.

The weekend of priestly ordination, first Mass and formal mission assignment was an important one for both Father Capodanno and his family. He expressed his gratitude to the Father General later in June: [57]

Dear Father General,

My ordination, impressed on my soul, is deep in my memory + will remain there, a source of many happy recollections.

I'd like to thank you for making it such a memorable weekend but especially I want to say thank you for your kindness, thoughtfulness + priestly ideal during the two years it was my privilege to live in the same house with you.

The ideal of the priesthood in a Maryknoller you set before us in your own life and in your conferences will always be an example to encourage me. I will strive to live up to the ideal of our Founders and ask that you keep me in your prayers lest these words remain only written + not lived.

The book you gave us, *Radiating Christ*, will be a great help in directing God's light to the shadows throughout the world.

My mother asks that I tell you how thankful + pleased she is about her enrollment as a perpetual member of Maryknoll.

I'm afraid, Father General, that my gratitude is feebly expressed, but it is sincerely felt + will be manifested by a special remembrance of you in my prayers.

---

[57] MFBA, Box: Capodanno Personnel Files. Folder: Capodanno, Rev. Vincent R/Documents, N.p. June 27, 1958, Vincent Capodanno, MM, to "Dear Father General" [handwritten, autographed].

Thank you again, Father, for all you have done for me + my classmates.

Respectfully grateful in Christ,

Vincent Capodanno.

Father Capodanno offered his first public Solemn Mass of Thanksgiving at his home parish of Our Lady of Good Counsel on Staten Island on June 22nd. Father Capodanno included a brief note inside the remembrance missal printed for the occasion:

My dear friends: My intention at this my first Solemn Mass is that God's blessings may fill your heart.

This little missal was written to help you understand some of the ceremonies and prayers of the Solemn Mass. The Church has surrounded the simple act of the early Christians, 'the breaking of the bread,' with many ceremonies that speak to man, body and soul, as he tries to praise God his creator. The perfect act of praise is the Mass. At the Last Supper Jesus took bread, blessed it and gave it to His Apostles, saying: 'Take and eat; this is my Body.' Then He took wine and blessed it saying: 'This is the Chalice of my Blood which shall be shed for you.' This was the first Mass.

The Mass is so important because it is the same Sacrifice of Christ on Calvary. Invisibly present at this Mass is Jesus, both high Priest and Victim. He offers Himself to His Father.

I share in Christ's priesthood. I want you to unite yourself with me as I offer this Mass. We as God's family have come together to praise our Father through Christ our Brother. [58]

---

[58] AMIL, Box: Seminarian and Missionary Album. Booklet: "The Holy Sacrifice of the Mass: Remembrance of the First Solemn Mass, Our Lady of Good Counsel Church, June 22, 1958."

Another Maryknoll missionary remembered meeting the newly-ordained Father Capodanno during the summer of 1958. Father James P. Nieckarz, MM, was a Maryknoll seminarian, studying at Glen Ellyn, and was working during the summer vacation as an orderly at Saint Vincent's Hospital on Staten Island.

One day, Father Capodanno was visiting the sick at the hospital, and the two men met. The young seminarian was happy to speak with the newly-ordained priest about Maryknoll and about his vocation to the priesthood. Father Nieckarz recalled,

> The fact that we were attracted to Maryknoll, which Gene Autry had referred to as the 'Marine Corps of the Catholic Church', might well have come up but at least our fascination with the call to missions + preaching the Gospel abroad in addition to a kind of romantic attraction to adventure + to the Orient were a common thread.

> But most of all I remember Father Capodanno had a certain aura of seriousness, intensity, yet he was approachable + not without a sense of humor about him. And even more impressive, there was a sense of a deeply spiritual character in Father Vincent.

> Over the years, when I talked about him to others, I've usually said, 'A deep spirituality seemed to ooze from him, which made his presence arresting.

> Father Vincent was ten years older than me + had just completed the nine years preparation for the priesthood that I was just beginning.

> He became a kind of hero + certainly a role model for me + I do recall thinking then + telling others later, 'I'd like to become a priest like Father Capodanno.'

> The positive impression I'm sure, supported my resolve to continue in Maryknoll during the remaining

eight years of my seminary days, often recalling that 'graceful' encounter with Father Vince.[59]

---

[59] AMIL, Box: Capodanno Personal Testimonies. Staten Island, July 12, 2006, Father James P. Nieckarz, MM, to Mary Preece.

Chapter II

Formosa and Language School

By 1949, the Communists were victorious in mainland China and Taiwan became the home of Nationalist China. Led by General Chiang Kai-shek, a government in exile was established with Taipei as its capital, welcoming exiles and political refugees, along with train loads of the best of the ancient art treasures that mainland China had produced, awaiting the time for the re-establishment of a free China. Following that Communist victory, waves of Catholic priests, religious and laity streamed to Taiwan seeking refuge on the island nation, which had been promised military protection by the United States of America.

The Maryknoll missions on the island were under the direction of two Maryknollers. Father William F. Kupfer, MM, had been assigned to the Apostolic Prefecture of Wuchow immediately after priestly ordination in 1933, and remained there for the next fourteen years. Bishop Frederick A. Donaghy, MM, had been named Vicar Apostolic of Wuchow, China, and consecrated bishop on September 21, 1939. Following imprisonment and torture by the Communist Chinese, Bishop Donaghy was expelled in 1955. Both Maryknoll men were seasoned missionaries, whose years in the Maryknoll mission field of China had produced extraordinary results as the Church developed on the mainland.

They now found themselves on the same island of Taiwan, but with roles somewhat reversed: Father Kupfer was named the Prefect Apostolic of Taichung when Rome created the mission territory January 13, 1951. While not a bishop, Father Kupfer exercised ordinary territorial jurisdiction as Prefect Apostolic; Bishop Donaghy, the former ordinary, now merely a titular bishop, performed two functions: exercising authority over the Maryknoll missioners in his region delegated by his Maryknoll superior, and was the local representative of the

Archbishop of Taipei.[60] Often, they would be at odds with each other, with contrasting opinions and policies about the Maryknoll missions, about the role of arriving Maryknoll missioners, and about the apportioning of Maryknoll funds.

Maryknoll was not the only Catholic missionary presence on Taiwan. On paper, the work of numerous Catholic missions of the various religious orders and congregations was impressive. The daily practicalities of overlapping responsibilities and jurisdictions made for uneven missionary work, however. One bothersome reality faced by the Maryknoll missioners offers a good example: the presence of a large and growing American population on Taiwan, resulting from the American military build-up after 1949. Father Kupfer wrote the Maryknoll Superior General on March 13, 1958 asking his guidance. He reported that several of the Maryknoll priests were spending "a good deal of time" with the Americans and English-speaking Filipinos, "with the result that their work among the natives has suffered." An American airbase was being built outside Taichung City, and the Catholic American military personnel along with their families, and the Catholic Filipino laborers building the airbase, all needed pastoral care. The question of jurisdiction for providing that care was complicated. Father Kupfer described the final arrangement:

> Fr. Pope has his jurisdiction as Pastor of the Americans from the Military Ordinariate. He has his jurisdiction as Rector of the district in the central part of Taichung City from me. Although in this central part he has jurisdiction over the Filipinos, he does not have jurisdiction over the natives in this same district.[61]

Into this growing yet complicated mission field arrived

---

[60] MFBA, Box 1: Taiwan Regional Records, Correspondence 1950-1959. Folder: Taiwan Records, 1/8, Regional Superior's Correspondence 1958. Maryknoll, NY, April 26, 1958, Father John W. Comber, MM, to Bishop Frederick A. Donaghy, MM.

[61] MFBA, Taiwan Regional Records, Correspondence 1950-1959, Box 1. Folder: Taiwan Records, 1/8, Regional Superior's Correspondence 1958. Taichung, Formosa, March 13, 1958, Father William F. Kupfer, MM, to "Father General."

the newly-ordained Father Vincent R. Capodanno, MM. Nearly one month after Father Vincent's ordination, Father Thomas J. Malone, MM, wrote Bishop Donaghy providing him with brief biographies of each new missionary soon to arrive in Taiwan. Father Malone had been Vincent's seminary rector, and wrote:

> Father Vincent R. Capodanno—is from Staten Island. He is a little older than the others—he is 29. He is quite capable in managing things. Would be able to get along on his own if it were necessary to put him out by himself. He should do fairly well in the language if he has patience enough to learn it correctly. He is a bit on the impetuous side and expects immediate results.[62]

It was Bishop Donaghy's decision to house Fathers Donald Sheehan and Vincent Capodanno with him at his residence in the town of Miaoli during their year-long study of the Hakka language.[63]

Each Maryknoll mission around the world was expected to maintain a mission diary. While Fathers Sheehan and Capodanno studied in Miaoli, they wrote the mission diary for the language school, alternating authorship each month. They offer an interesting real-time perspective of the life in Miaoli as seen by two young and enthusiastic priests, and are worth quoting extensively. Their mission diaries also express the innocence of these young American priests on their first venture outside the United States. Their primary duty was to study the local language. But the year was also one of their acculturation to their new life and new identities as priests in a mission world. Their writings during their first year in Miaoli are filled with reflections about their studies in the language school, and daily

---

[62] MFBA, Taiwan Regional Records Correspondence, 1950-1959, Box 1. Folder: Taiwan Records 1/8, Regional Superior's Correspondence 1958. Maryknoll, July 11, 1958, Father Thomas J. Malone, MM, to Bishop Frederick A. Donaghy, MM.

[63] MFBA, Taiwan Regional Records Correspondence, 1950-1959, Box 1. Folder: Taiwan Records 1/8, Regional Superior's Correspondence 1958. N. p. July 3, 1958, Bishop Frederick A. Donaghy, MM, to Father John W. Comber, MM.

life in Miaoli, along with observations of the annual round of Catholic and pagan cultural events. Each month's diary entry reported both the regular and extraordinary activities in the mission. For instance, the Maryknoll missioners from the neighboring towns met each month in Miaoli at the Maryknoll Center House for Eucharistic adoration and devotions. Other occasions, such as anniversaries of priestly ordination, dedications of new churches, or great public devotional celebrations, provided opportunities for the two young Maryknoll language students to become acquainted with the Maryknoll missioners on Taiwan.

Father Sheehan is the author of the September entries in the language school diary. His first entry, dated September 7, 1958, tells the story of the arrival of six Maryknollers—including Father Capodanno—at Taipei airport, after a long ocean voyage from the United States and ten days' delay in Japan. Local Maryknollers met them at the airport, and brought them to the Maryknoll house in Taipei, where they offered Mass and ate lunch. Fathers Sheehan and Capodanno were then brought by Father Rhodes, MM, to the town of Miaoli, "in Bishop Donaghy's station wagon."[64] Father Sheehan recorded, "Our arrival was heralded with the traditional fire-cracker salute, and a get-together of the Maryknollers living within a reasonable distance." He continued,

> The Maryknoll house here in Miaoli is situated next door to a pagan temple. Fr. Capodanno and I were both initiated into the life in the Orient right from the beginning. With the 'luck of the Irish', our arrival coincided with a festival at the temple. And so, it was serenaded [sic] into the early hours of the morning with the strident cacophony of Chinese music, and all the

---

[64] MFBA, Box 18: Taiwan Diaries. Folder: Diaries/Taiwan/Taichung Center House/Taichung Lang. School/ 1953-1958. Taichung, Taiwan, October 8, 1958, Father Joseph A. Kimmerling, MM, to Father Collins, MM. See Appendix I for the complete diary entries.

hoop-la that goes hand-in-hand with a Chinese festival. The pagan temple next door, incidentally, is owned by Maryknoll. Bishop Donaghy proudly claims to be the only Catholic Bishop in the world to own a pagan temple. Lest erstwhile Canon lawyers fall over each other rushing to the *Code* or to the *Fontes*, let it be said that the temple itself is to be moved—it is the property that the Bishop of Wuchow purchased for Maryknoll.[65]

The two young American priests registered their first impressions of the town of Miaoli—which would prove a center of civilization and technological progress, compared with the isolated villages to which they would be assigned after completing their language studies. These young men were born and raised in the United States in relative luxury compared with the rest of the post war world. Now, for the first time, not only were they outside their home country, they were in a world that was politically and militarily volatile on an international scale, yet relatively primitive on the level of daily existence. It is important to take into consideration the radical changes they faced after years of relative solitude, relative comfort and tranquility in Maryknoll's seminary in Ossining, New York. Father Sheehan described them well:

> Neophyte missioners down through the years are all, I am sure, duly moved with initial impressions of the mission country where they are to labor. Frs. Capodanno and Sheehan are no exception to this, but would be embarrassed to mention what initially made the biggest impression on them—the humidity! Whether the humidity or the 'bed' situation made the biggest impression, is controversial. Having spent two years on promotion work in sunny Southern California, the writer mistakenly thought this would prepare him for the

---

[65] MFBA, Taiwan Diaries, Box 18. Folder 23: Taiwan-Taipei-Miaoli Language School 1954-1960. Father Donald J. Sheehan, MM, "Language School Diaries, <u>September, 1958</u>," pp. 1-2. See Appendix I.

tropics. Let me hasten to correct that impression for anyone else so similarly misinformed. It is not true. No sooner than it took to place our bags down, than we were hastening to invest in two electric fans. Even with the mechanical aid furnished by such a convenience, you find yourself soaked with perspiration from just standing—or sitting or doing nothing.

Something else that impressed me, I would label generically under the category of 'noise'. Noise is common all over the world, but I do believe an Oriental town has more than its share. From long before dawn, till the wee hours of the morning, there is a constant din. There is the usual crow of the rooster, bark of the dog, toot of the horn, and cry of children. But add to these the sound of radios blaring out at top volume from small shops along the street, and the rumbling of carts being pulled by water-buffalo on the road beyond the gate, or the rhythmical cadence of wooden clogs on hard pavement. All joined together, this makes a very vivid first impression, albeit I must confess it has already become commonplace to me, and I now take it for granted.

Before beginning their studies, the two priests visited the missions in the Miaoli territory. Father Sheehan commented on the development of the Church in the area:

When you recall that just five years ago, when Fr. Hilbert and Fr. Glass first arrived in Miaoli, there were no Catholics and no buildings of any sort, you cannot help but be impressed by the progress that has been made. In the town of Miaoli itself, Fr. Hilbert and Fr. Madigan have flourishing parishes, caring for over a thousand Catholics. With few exceptions, the larger towns and villages within the area of Miaoli are all cared for ably by Maryknollers.

Father Capodanno wrote the diary entries for October, 1958.[66] He described the various public Marian devotions, and the visit to local missions by the two young priests. On October 10th, the day after the death of Pope Pius XII,

> We joined the rest of the world in praying for the repose of his soul. The Generalissimo [Chiang Kai-shek] ordered all public buildings to fly their flags at half-mast for three days beginning Sunday, October 12.
>
> Later that same afternoon Bishop Donaghy returned from his visitation to Hong Kong. He was met at the front gate by his two barking dogs, who live here under Episcopal patronage, and by his two smiling language students.
>
> We had supper with Fr. Don McGinnis and then attended October Devotions in his temporary church. The faces of many pagan children peered thru the open windows as they stared unintelligbly [sic] at the ceremonies. The bars on the windows seemed to accent their present exclusion from Mater Ecclesia.

Besides the monthly mission diary, the local regional superior penned his own monthly reports. By the end of October, Bishop Donaghy wrote the Maryknoll Father General that:

> The two new priests, Fathers Sheehan and Capodanno, are living with me in the old manse, we have our meals in the new house, and the director of the language school, Father Hilbert is very satisfied with the progress they are making. They both appear to be fine types, happy to be on the missions and keenly interested in everything that is

---

[66] MFBA, Taiwan Diaries, Box 18. Folder 23: Taiwan-Taipei-Miaoli Language School 1954-1960. Father Vincent R. Capodanno, MM, "Language School Diaries for <u>October, 1958,</u>" p. 1. See Appendix I.

going on.[67]

As he became more engrossed in his language studies, Father Vincent had less time to answer the growing number of letters from friends and family. He found the most productive way to manage his correspondence was by composing form letters, which he would write throughout his years of priestly ministry, usually accompanied by handwritten messages to the recipients. He kept up an enormous written correspondence using form letters to provide supplemental, usually non-personal details. In his *A Note from Miaoli* form letter, he described the ocean crossing from Wilmington, California to the missions that began on August 8, 1958. He also gave his own perspective of the town of Miaoli on the verso of the form letter he sent his friend, George Driscoll:

> Miaoli is a small oriental rural town with one main street. Actually, in some respects it is not too unlike some small Western towns. I spend my days studying the language. It isn't the hardest language in the world but neither is it the easiest! Oriental—at least Chinese—languages use tones; if you don't use the right tone you're not saying what you intend to! However it is coming along. Keep me in your prayers, George, + always count on a very special remembrance in mine.[68]

On November 10th, an extraordinary event took place in the small town with the visit to Miaoli of Archbishop Anthony Riberi and the Brazilian ambassador to Taiwan. Archbishop Riberi had been the papal internuncio to China, recently imprisoned and expelled by the Communist Chinese. He spoke to the two young Maryknoll priests about one of the great Maryknoll missionaries, Bishop Francis Xavier Ford, MM, who

---

[67] MFBA, Taiwan Regional Records, Correspondence 1950-1959, Box 1. Folder: Taiwan Records 1/8, Regional Superior's Correspondence 1958. Miaoli, Taiwan, October 28, 1958, Bishop Frederick A. Donaghy, MM, to "Father General."

[68] AMIL, Box: Correspondence Binder. *A Note from Miaoli*, October, 1958, Father Vincent R. Capodanno, MM, to George T. Driscoll.

died of starvation and years of maltreatment at the hands of the communists in 1952. Father Sheehan commented: "To hear another Maryknoller praised so highly by a Churchman in a position such as Archbishop Riberi's [sic], makes one extremely proud to be able to wear a Maryknoll Chi-Rho on his cincture."[69]

On December 18, 1958, the young missionaries left Miaoli to spend their first Christmas in a Maryknoll mission, in the village of Tahu, whose pastor was Father Lloyd Glass, MM. On December 24th, Father Sheehan remained in town with the curate, Father Chu, MM, while Father Capodanno ventured into the mountains with Father Glass to the smaller Our Lady of Lourdes mission chapel, ". . . built by and for the Aborigines."[70] After the priests helped string outdoor Christmas lights and connected them to a generator, the festivities began. Father Capodanno continued his narrative:

> The setting was a small gully, actually the mountain road, in front of the chapel. The festivity was a series of races of men, women and children, and also the two Fathers. Everyone spent the morning racing, singing, laughing and in general having a good time.
>
> After dinner and a few more hours of singing and talking, about two hundred people crowded into the small chapel for a game of bingo. Since the Blessed Sacrament is not reserved in the chapel, and since there is no other building around, Fr. Glass draws a curtain across the sanctuary and permits the parishioners to use the rest of the chapel as a social room. The prizes lasted about an hour and then they began to clean up the chapel while the pastor heard confessions and the visiting assistant slept.

---

[69] MFBA, Taiwan Diaries, Box 18. Folder 33: Taiwan-Taipei-Miaoli Language School, 1958-1959. Father Donald J. Sheehan, MM, "Miaoli Language School, November 1958," pg. 2. See Appendix I.

[70] MFBA, Taiwan Diaries, Box 18. Folder 33: Taiwan-Taipei-Miaoli Language School, 1958-1959. Father Vincent R. Capodanno, MM, "Miaoli Language School Diary, December, 1958," p. 1. See Appendix I.

The Aborigines are a colorful, friendly, intelligent people who may not have much material wealth but who do have a spirit of independence. That trait showed itself by the fact that they kept their children home from school and that they arranged on their own all the activities of the day, including the prizes given out.

Just before I began Midnight Mass, the men lined the side aisles of the chapel with straw and in a few minutes the very young and the very old were stretched out fast asleep. The Manger next to the altar seemed very much at home.

After Mass, which they sang in excellent Latin, they sang some more while I said my second Mass. Later on, those who lived too far to walk home and return for the morning Masses, spread more straw on the floor and slept in the chapel.

Outside, a full moon lit up the sky and somewhere a mountain waterfall roared its alleluia for the Birthday of the King.

About 5 A.M. yours truly rolled over in his sleeping-bag while the aborigines cleaned the chapel and sang Christmas carols around a bonfire made from the straw.

After Fr. Glass said his three Masses and I said my final Mass, everyone went home except a small group who busied themselves cleaning the chapel and the yard.

An hour's ride over the same bumps and we were back in Tahu where Frs. Chu and Sheehan celebrated their Christmas Masses for the townspeople and some of the near-by Aborigines.

One turkey dinner and a bus ride later, we were back in Miaoli where business and school went on as usual. One of the parishes put on a play at a local theatre that evening and if the pagans didn't know why, they at least knew that the Catholics gathered together to celebrate something.

The clergy of Miaoli Deanery gathered together on the 26th for a Christmas party, and after a weekend of visiting and being visited the doors of the language school swung open for class on Monday morning. Wednesday brings the first day of a four day holiday and the last day of 1958.

Even in a few short months we have been here the Church has noticeably grown in numbers and so on New Year's Eve, 1958 we return thanks to God for His many graces here in Miaoli and pray for the continued expansion of His Kingdom, here and thru [sic] the world.

In his January form letter to his family and friends, Father Capodanno provided more details about his Christmas work in the mountain mission:

On Christmas Eve they played various family games, one of which was a series of races. I was looking at the scenery, when I heard some one yelling, 'Ka Sin fou'— my Chinese name (pronounced GA SIN FOO). Before I knew what was happening a fleet-footed Aborigine boy was dragging me along. When I realized I was in a race I put my effort in the running + we came in first. What happened was that 5 racers run to a point + pick up a card on which is written an object they must bring back to the starting line. While I was running I turned around once to see who was at my heels. I nearly fell when I saw another boy holding the hand of an old woman. There she was, barefoot, tatooes [sic] on her face + a pipe in her mouth. She laughed, puffed on her pipe. but all the while kept the pace set by her young partner! Just for the record—she came in <u>second</u>.

I offered one of my Christmas Masses for all of you.

I always remember you in my prayers + every Mass I pray for my friends + the people who mean a great deal to me.[71]

The first winter for Father Capodanno was a typical one on Taiwan: cold and gray.[72] As is obvious from the letters and diary entries by both Fathers Sheehan and Capodanno, they preferred to be engaged in pastoral work in the mission parishes, but they obediently continued on with their assigned duty studying the Hakka language. As Bishop Donaghy reported, "The language students all appeared in fine spirits and singularly free of the *anui* [sic] usually complained of at this time of year."[73]

Father Capodanno returned to the mountains on March 25, 1959 to assist the local Maryknoll pastor during Holy Week and Easter. On Easter Sunday he traveled with the pastor to outlying mountain chapels to offer

> . . . Easter Mass with the Aborigines. We couldn't have Mass on Easter at each of the five mountain chapels so some of the people had to walk over a few mountains but they didn't mind.
>
> I climbed up half a mountain to reach one of the chapels + stopped many times on the way to admire the scenery, of course! I was carrying nothing but a walking stick. The residents of 'them thar' hills' usually have heavy packs strapped to their backs or resting on their backs with all the weight pulling on a strap across the

---

[71] AMIL, Box: Correspondence Binder. Miaoli, Taiwan, January 10, 1959, Father Vincent R. Capodanno, MM, to George T. Driscoll.

[72] MFBA, Taiwan Diaries, Box 18. Folder: 33: Taiwan-Taipei-Miaoli Language School, 1958-1959. Father Donald L. Sheehan, MM, "Language School Diary, Miaoli, January 1959," p. 1. See Appendix I.

[73] MFBA, Taiwan Regional Records Reports to General Council 1952-1990; Visitations 1950-1988, Box 7. Folder: Taiwan Records 7/2, Regional Superior's Reports to General Council 1954-1962. Formosa, March 1959, Bishop Frederick Donaghy, MM: "Monthly Diary of Regional Superior, March 1959."

forehead![74]

April brought with it the annual celebration of the birth of a local pagan deity, called *Mat su*, known as the "Queen of Heaven." In his monthly diary entry, Father Capodanno repeated local theories that the pagan worship had its roots in earlier local Catholic devotion to the Blessed Mother: ". . . an incomplete devotion to Mary was incorporated into the pagan religious life of fishermen and gradually grew in popularity while it was being warped into its present shape." He continued describing the local pagan procession:

> The air was heavy with the dull booms of drums, loud explosions and firecrackers, piercing clangs of cymbals and shrill blasts of flutes but even more noticeable was the presence of something negative. There was no joy. There was confusion, noise, incense, but no real joy; just a long line of people beating out their devotion to a non-existent deity. *Mat su* has come and gone and Miaoli will settle itself down to its ordinary daily life.[75]

By mid-May, 1959, "the Island of Formosa became formosior" ["more beautiful" as Father Sheehan quipped].[76] For the Feast of Corpus Christi, May 28th, the two language students were employed in nearby missions: Father Capodanno preached in Chinese for the first time at the parish in the town of Tunglo, to which he would be assigned after he completed his

---

[74] AMIL, Box: Correspondence Binder. Miaoli Catholic Mission Office, March 30, 1959, Father Capodanno, MM, to Mr. & Mrs. George T. Driscoll and Family.

[75] MFBA, Taiwan Diaries, Box 18. Folder 33: Taiwan-Taipei-Miaoli Language School 1958-1959. Father Vincent R. Capodanno, MM, "Miaoli Language School Diary, April 1959," pp. 3-4. See Appendix I.

[76] MFBA, Taiwan Diaries, Box 18. Folder 33: Taiwan-Taipei-Miaoli Language School, 1958-1959. Father Donald L. Sheehan, MM, "Miaoli Language School Diary, May, 1959," p. 1. See Appendix I.

language studies in late June.[77]

The two student priests were ready to enter true mission work. Father Sheehan gave an idea of their eagerness to enter pastoral work as their language studies were drawing to a close:

> The end of May finds the two language students hanging bravely on for the last month of language school. The feeling is something similar to the grit and determination that one musters up in the dentist's chair, as the dentist gives the last, whirring bore with his drill (so close to the nerve!) prior to filling a cavity in a tooth. You know its [sic] necessary, but you're so happy to see him push the drill away. We look for the drill being pushed away on June 29th, Foundation Day.

Father Capodanno wrote the final diary entry of June for that year's language student priests, who were in high spirits as they completed their studies:

> Fr. Hilbert now relinquishes the helm he has held for these past nine months to the two new graduates and [to] the teachers they will have in their new parishes. Our thanks to Fr. Hilbert lies in the fact that we have already both preached twice [in the Hakka language] and feel confident to go to many more sermons.
>
> We bade farewell to the [broken] glass-topped walls of the Miaoli language school, the scene of the first phase of the language battle but also the scene of a pleasant year with Bishop Donaghy, Fr. Rhodes, Fr. Wu and Brother Pascal. Lest the Bishop find the house too quiet while he is here alone, we leave him with one parakeet, fifteen goldfish, one cat, two dogs and

[77] MFBA, Taiwan Regional Records, Correspondence 1950-1959, Box 1. Folder: Taiwan Records, 1/9, Regional Superior's Correspondence 1959, Jan-Sept. Miaoli, June 2, 1959, Bishop Frederick A. Donaghy, MM, to Most Reverend John W. Comber, MM.

six new puppies.[78]

Each Maryknoll regional superior filed an annual personnel report. Bishop Donaghy rated Father Capodanno as consistently "good" [the categories were "good," "fair" or "poor"] for each of the standard questions concerning each missioner, which included his physical and spiritual health, whether he dressed in accord with the Maryknoll directives, his spirit of poverty [in accord with article 264 of the Maryknoll Constitutions], his hospitality to other Maryknollers, his visiting of his confrères in other missions, his attitude toward the people he served, and his spoken ability in the Hakka language. The report noted that Father Capodanno had not been absent for more than one week at any time during the previous year, and that he was "contented" in his attitude toward the present assignment. Under the heading, "Brief estimate of the mission and his work," Bishop Donaghy wrote that Father Capodanno was a:

> Cordial, affable type, very popular with all the priests, rather meticulous in dress, food and living quarters but [I] feel he will gradually adapt himself to conditions on the missions. He studied hard and faithfully and obtained quite a good grasp on the language.[79]

Father Capodanno's habits of personal hygiene and dress seemed to annoy Bishop Donaghy, however, for he repeatedly mentioned them in his reports. His personal habits seemed to set Father Capodanno apart from some of the other older Maryknoll missionaries, who had been expelled from mainland China and were working on Taiwan. Father J. Donald McGinnis, MM, a friend of Father Capodanno on Taiwan at the time, offered an

---

[78] MFBA, Taiwan Diaries, Box 18. Folder 33: Taiwan-Taipei-Miaoli Language School, 1958-1959. Father Vincent R. Capodanno, MM" Miaoli Language School Diary, June 1959," pp. 1-2. See Appendix I.

[79] MFBA, Box: Capodanno Personnel File. Folder: Capodanno, Rev. Vincent R/Documents. Bishop Frederick A. Donaghy, MM, Personnel Report: July 1, 1958 to June 30, 1959. Priests on Mission, July 15, 1959.

interesting perspective:

> I was in Miaoli County, Taiwan when Vince [Capodanno] arrived. One quality that stands out was that he was always neat, always well-groomed. This stood out because others [Maryknoll missioners] thought it was 'macho', 'rugged' to be somewhat indifferent to their dress and appearance. Vince was able to keep this gift even when he worked in the mountains with the aborigine people—and real remote, somewhat isolated and a work always done on foot.[80]

The priest language students received their mission assignments from Bishop Donaghy. After a brief vacation in Hong Kong the two priests reported to their new pastors: Father Sheehan to Father Lloyd Glass, MM, in the mission in Tahu, and Father Capodanno to Father Maynard Murphy, MM, in the mission in Tunglo.[81] "I'm sure Father Sheehan and Capodanno are happy to have completed the language course and to get into the active work," wrote Father Clarence Witte, MM, Mission Secretary at Maryknoll. "There is plenty for them to do, and Fathers Glass and Murphy will probably keep them busy enough."[82]

---

[80] AMIL, Box: Correspondence Personal Testimonies. Taipei, February 22, 2007, Father J. Donald McGinnis, MM, to "Dear Roberta."

[81] MFBA, Taiwan Regional Records Correspondence 1950-1959, Box 1. Folder: Taiwan Records 1/9, Regional Superior's Correspondence 1959, Jan-Sept. Miaoli, June 28, 1959, Bishop Frederick A. Donaghy, MM, to Father Clarence Witte, MM.

[82] MFBA, Ibid. Maryknoll, NY, July 10, 1959, Very Reverend Clarence Witte, MM, to Bishop Frederick A. Donaghy, MM.

Chapter III

The Missions in Tunglo and Miaoli

Father Capodanno moved to his first mission assignment at Saint Mary's Parish in the mountain town of Tunglo. He was then allowed to take his annual vacation at the Maryknoll house in Hong Kong during the first weeks of August, 1959. The vacation time in Hong Kong included pastoral work for the young priest, for it offered him his first introduction to working with the United States Navy. After briefly describing Hong Kong and the Maryknoll work for refugees in the Crown Colony, the young missioner wrote to his friend George Driscoll about Maryknoll's work for American servicemen:

> On the other hand, there are many tourists running to + fro, among them crews from the ships in our Seventh Fleet. It was a wide open liberty port for many years + not too long ago the sailors would be gypped, robbed + beaten almost as soon as they stepped on land. A Maryknoll priest organized what is now known as Seaman's Wharf. It has a big sign 'For God + For Country' that seems to set the theme of the work. Tours are arranged; lists of reliable stores have been drawn up; a snack bar + money-changing booth are open from dawn to dawn; there is always a Catholic + a Protestant chaplain on the premises. Things have changed + now American sailors go home with much happiness + memories of Hong Kong.
>
> I used to go out to the ships for confessions + Mass on Sunday mornings. It was a very pleasant + enjoyable part of my vacation.[83]

Father Capodanno's vacation in Hong Kong spared him from the five days of flooding and landslides on Taiwan that

---

[83] AMIL, Box: Correspondence Binder. Tunglo, November 27, 1959, Father Vincent R. Capodanno, MM, to George T. Driscoll.

began on the night of August 7th, the worst in fifty years. By the time he returned to Tunglo, the cleanup had begun. He wrote his friend,

> The pastor told me there was [sic] a few inches of water in the chapel + rectory but outside it was about 2 feet deep! Most of the people killed died in landslides. It all happened during the night + from what I have heard, the worst landslides were very sudden. Some mountain sides look like they have huge rivers of stone flowing down.
>
> Many rice paddies were covered with mud + others buried under tons of rock. It will be a long time before these farmers recover the financial loss.
>
> Catholic Relief + American relief began on the morning after the flood. Besides the material help, the idea that someone was giving food helped keep the people from panicing [sic].[84]

Incomplete reports estimated 800 dead; 500 missing; 1,000 injured, with more than 180,000 flood victims. 30,000 homes were completely or partially destroyed; 200 bridges washed away, severe damage to crops and to roads, rails and telegraphic communications. [85] The Chinese [Taiwanese] and United States Air Force, local and national police, and the local Catholic Church joined forces with American Catholic Relief Services—the National Catholic Welfare Conference—and sent 700 tons of dried milk, flour and corn meal. The Maryknoll missioners directed most of the relief work on the island, cooperating with the United States Marines. Monsignor William Kupfer, MM, reported the relief efforts:

> Fifteen U.S. Marine helicopters on the ship [USS *Thetis*

---

[84] AMIL, Box: Correspondence Binder. Tunglo Mission, October 9, 1959, Father Vincent R. Capodanno, MM, to George T. Driscoll.

[85] *Mission Bulletin*, November 1959, vol. XI, No. 8, p. 987.

Bay, from Hong Kong] carried more than 1,600,540 pounds of supplies in 897 flights to the stricken areas. Maryknoll Fathers in the disaster area directed the helicopters to places where the food was needed and then helped load the sick and injured on the helicopters for flights to hospitals and other medical centers.[86]

In an effort to assist the people of the Miaoli Deanery, Bishop Donaghy purchased large industrial-sized noodle and quilt making machines from Hong Kong to be installed in a rented building in Miaoli. He wrote his superiors, "Once produced, the noodles will have a much greater appeal to the poor than the raw flour and corn meal previously distributed; and the quilts will be most welcome to the many who lost all their possessions in the August flood."[87]

As Tunglo worked to restore normalcy to daily life after the floods, Father Capodanno was entrusted to keep the mission diary. His pastor, Father Maynard Murphy, MM, had worked for years to build up a thriving parish, with great success. By the time Father Capodanno arrived in Tunglo in late summer of 1959, plans were well developed to rent a small shop, to repair and furnish it to serve as a Catholic library for the town. A banquet celebrating the completion of the new library was held on October 14; the pastor blessed and officially opened the library on October 18. Father Capodanno wrote about the new library: "Through it we hope to disperse Catholic literature to those who have no inclination to come to the parish itself."[88]

The pastor of the mission in Tunglo was leaving for a

---

[86] *Mission Bulletin*, December 1959, vol. XI, No. 9, pp. 1092-1093.

[87] MFBA, Taiwan Regional Records Reports to General Council 1952-1990, Visitations 1950-1988, Box 7. Folder: Taiwan Records 7/2 Regional Superior's Reports to General Council 1954-1962. Bishop Frederick A. Donaghy, MM: "Monthly Diary of Regional Superior: Formosa Region, November 1959," p. 1r.

[88] MFBA, Capodanno Personnel File, Box 12. Folder 2: Tunglo Diary, 1959. Father Vincent R. Capodanno, MM, "Tunglo Diary Digest September and October 1959," p 2. See Appendix I.

scheduled furlough, provided periodically by Maryknoll for their missioners. Finding himself finally in an active mission after one year of language school, Father Capodanno added a postscript to his mission diary entry, reflecting on the work of his fellow missionaries in general, and on Father Murphy in particular:

> I am going to add a P.S. to this diary in the form of a personal reflection. As Maryknoll grows in numbers and mission territories it becomes more difficult to follow the activities of all members. Some men will stand out in the future as others have in the past. They are well known, or will be, and justly receive acclaim for what we might term famous work. In contrast to them, there will be in the future as there is now another group who have done their work faithfully and well but who are practically unknown. Their work has never made the headlines, but without their work Maryknoll would not achieve its purpose. Yet, if their names are mentioned outside their own region they are either vaguely recognized or totally unknown. Their number will increase with time; their fame, never.

> Those were the thoughts of a neophyte missioner as he bid bon voyage [sic] to a very fine pastor who was returning home for a brief time; for the fourth brief time in thirty-two consecutive years.[89]

While the pastor of the Tunglo mission was on furlough in the United States, Father Daniel Dolan, MM, took over as temporary pastor on November 6th, with Father Capodanno serving as his curate.

Father Capodanno's days were occupied with mission work in the town of Tunglo and its two neighboring villages, and with continued study of the Hakka language. "I prefer the

---

[89] MFBA, Capodanno Personnel File, Box 12. Folder 2: Tunglo Diary, 1959. Father Vincent R. Capodanno, MM, "Tunglo Diary Digest September and October 1959," p. 4. See Appendix I.

mission work but the language study is its necessary adjunct."[90] The total population of the town was about 6,000 people, of which 199 were Catholics, "but almost twice that number have taken instructions, requested and received Baptism."[91] Once baptized, many moved away to other areas of Taiwan in search of work.

Father Capodanno and Father Dolan also visited two small villages "deep in from the main roads." In one, they offered Mass and gave instructions in the faith inside a tiny shop. In the other town, they used a room in one of the mud and straw houses. They also taught catechists every day, who would then go to the smaller villages to give instructions in the faith. The total Catholic population in both towns was 50 Catholics. "The number of Catholics in Tunglo may not be spectacular, but the Church is planted and will continue to grow," Father Capodanno wrote in the mission diary.

The recently-opened Catholic library was having success among the native population, with growing numbers of daily visitors, both Catholic and pagan. There was a series of posters in the library that attracted the attention of newcomers, who asked questions about the faith. During November and December, Father Capodanno devised two new series of posters for the library. One series was about the Mass, the other about Christmas and the Incarnation, using pictures that appeared in parish Sunday bulletins from the United States. Father Capodanno continued in the diary,

> Since we are changing the poster each day the question of appropriate pictures would have been a great one. The complete set will cover all the main Old Testament themes necessary for an understanding of Christmas, if such a thing be possible in one month's time. A caption in

---

[90] CAP/Staten, Tunglo, Christmas, 1959, Father Vincent R. Capodanno, MM, to Mr. + Mrs. A. Ishill, "A Note from Tunglo," p. 1.

[91] CAP/Staten, Ibid.

Chinese characters helps fill in the gaps.[92]

Among the steady patrons of the Catholic library were some young pagan men. They had completed school but were unemployed, waiting to be inducted into the Taiwanese army. As Father Capodanno wrote:

> They comprise the Catholic Church English classes presented twice a week at the library. This was their first personal contact with the Church and to create a stronger tie, they were invited to form themselves into a volleyball team to represent the Tunglo mission at games with other Catholic missions.[93]

Father Capodanno named the team the "Tunglo Tigers," and they entered into competition with the Maryknoll mission in Yuan Li in mid-December. The Catholic teams from Yuan Li arrived in Tunglo on December 12th, and were soundly beaten by Father Capodanno's "all-pagan Tunglo teams." "Grace builds on nature," was Father's comment about his team's victory and his creative efforts to convert the pagans.[94]

Christmas preparations included erecting elaborate decorations around the mission church and throughout the town, and providing free informational pamphlets about the meaning of Christmas, distributed to all who wanted them, especially through the Catholic library. Father Vincent quipped, "The gates of the church were not broken down by crowds of pagans trying to come in for Christmas Mass, but everyone in Tunglo knew it was Christmas, and more important, knew also the meaning of the Birth of Christ."[95]

---

[92] MFBA, Capodanno Personnel Files, Box 12, Folder 2: Tunglo Diary, 1959. Father Vincent R. Capodanno, MM, "Tunglo Diary, <u>November, 1959</u>," p. 3. See Appendix I.

[93] MFBA, Ibid.

[94] MFBA, Capodanno Personnel Files, Box 12. Folder 2: Tunglo Diaries, 1959. Father Vincent R. Capodanno, M, "Tunglo Diary, <u>December, 1959</u>," p. 1. See Appendix I.

[95] MFBA, Ibid.

Father Capodanno concluded his diary entries for the year, writing, "1959 closes with a cold dark day, which in no way symbolizes the bright hopes for the growth of the Chruch [sic] in Tunglo, one of the many Nazareths of Taiwan."[96]

The annual report of the Maryknoll Miaoli Deanery, prepared by Bishop Donaghy for the Archdiocese of Taipei, revealed the statistics of Saint Mary's Parish in Tunglo for 1959. The number of Catholics on June 30, 1958 totaled 152. During the year, there had been 30 adult baptisms and 6 infant baptisms. There was a decrease by 14 persons, because of death or moving away from Tunglo. By June 30, 1959, the total number of Catholics was 174 persons.[97]

Throughout his years of priestly ministry, Father Capodanno remembered his family in his daily Masses and prayers, and offered one Mass each week specifically for their intentions. Part of his active ministry was his correspondence. He regularly received letters, cards, gifts of food and clothing and spiritual bouquets from his family and friends, and he did his best to type personal notes of gratitude in response.[98] Frequently, especially in response to news of a family marriage, birth or death, he offered beautiful meditations.[99]

Father Capodanno also wrote home, describing scenes of life of Tunglo:

> Yesterday, today and tomorrow mark the middle of the first month of the New Chinese Year. This is the traditional end of the New Year celebrations + vacation—

---

[96] Ibid.

[97] MFBA, Taiwan Regional Records, Box 1. Folder 10: Miaoli Deanery Annual Report, 1959. "Maryknoll Miaoli Deanery, Archdiocese of Taipei Annual Report for 1959."

[98] AMIL, Box: Correspondence Binder. N.p. [Tunglo?], February 12, 1960, Father Vincent R. Capodanno, MM, to Pauline, George, George + Vin; Tunglo, April 22, 1960, Father Vincent R. Capodanno, MM, to Mr. + Mrs. E. Kaufman.

[99] AMIL, Box: Correspondence Binder. N.p. [Tunglo?], May 31, 1960, Father Vincent R. Capodanno, MM, to Kathleen.

school opens Monday. This is the season of the dragon parade + the Lantern Festival. Even Tunglo had a dragon parade! We contributed $30.00 [Taiwanese] toward the making of the dragon + since that was the largest contribution in Tunglo we got a special bow as the dragon went past last night. I forgot to buy fire crackers yesterday but did buy them today. You are supposed to set them off as the dragon approaches. We had them all ready tonight but the dragon never came—some one threw a fire cracker + it landed on the dragon + part of it burned! They repaired it + now I can here [sic] the drums, cymbals + more firecrackers as the parade winds its way thru [sic] the streets and alleys.

Usually the dragon first goes to the pagan temple + worships the idols. I had to make sure the Tunglo dragon was just going through the streets before I gave the money. The boys who were going to carry it said 'No Temple for us' + I don't think they did go.[100]

By the end of his first year in Tunglo, Father Capodanno received a good evaluation from his regional superior. The only criticism made by Bishop Donaghy characterized Father Capodanno's writing skills in Hakka as "weak," even though his spoken and reading abilities were good.[101] Bishop Donaghy also noted that "He seemed to manifest a special facility in dealing with young people and it was decided to put him in charge of the Hostel for High School boys to be opened in Miaoli this Fall."[102]

Bishop Donaghy planned to open two youth hostels in the Miaoli area: one for high school girls, directed by a religious sister, and one for high school boys, directed by a priest. This

---

[100] AMIL, Box: Correspondence Binder. n.p. Tunglo, February 12, 1960, Father Vincent R. Capodanno, MM, to Pauline.

[101] MFBA, Box: Capodanno Personnel File; Folder: Capodanno, Rev. Vincent R/Document. N.p., August 23, 1960, Bishop Frederick A. Donaghy, MM: "Personnel Report, Priests on Mission. Period: July 1, 1959 to June 30, 1960," p. 1r.

[102] MFBA, Ibid., p. 1v.

decision was the fruit of the various suggestions by the Bishop to his Maryknoll superiors made in late 1959, in an effort to extend the Church's influence in Taiwan culture and to increase the number of converts to the faith. He asked permission to open new primary schools, and requested more priests and religious sisters who could establish new missions outside the larger towns among the Aboriginal peoples. Both requests were refused. [103]

There had been two catechetical schools in the Miaoli Region, but the territory was too small to support both. His decision to open the hostels appeared to be an effective one, since within only two weeks of opening the girls' hostel, there were six girls under instruction for the faith. The Bishop described the theory behind the opening of the hostels:

> The students are encouraged to bring their classmates along for a visit and recreation and in this manner we hope to make many contacts in the school. Father McCabe has made available two large rooms in his Catholic Center for students who wish a quiet place in the evenings to do their homework away from the hubbub of a busy household and this has proven very popular with the young men; he presently has some fifty odd taking advantage of this and is now planning how to make more room available.[104]

Father Capodanno's talents were thought to fit the needs of this new effort, and so he was named House Superior of the

---

[103] MFBA, Taiwan Regional Records, Correspondence 1950-1959, Box 1. Folder: Taiwan Records 1/10, Regional Superior's Correspondence 1959, Oct.-Dec. Miaoli, November 15, 1959, Bishop Frederick A. Donaghy, MM, to Rev. Clarence Witte, MM; MFBA, same reference: Miaoli, December 10, 1959, Bishop Frederick A. Donaghy, MM, to Most Rev. John W. Comber, MM.

[104] MFBA, Taiwan Regional Records Reports to General Council 1952-1990, Visitations 1950-1988 Box 7. Folder: Taiwan Records 7/2 Regional Superior's Reports to General Council 1954-1962. Formosa Region. Bishop Frederick A. Donaghy, MM, "Monthly Diary of Regional Superior, September, 1960," p. 1r.

Miaoli Maryknoll Center House and Director of the Boys' Student Hostel.[105] There was need for someone with an engaging personality who could win over pagan youths to the Catholic faith, to counter the contrary pressures from their families, and the occasional counter-Catholic efforts of Protestant ministers. Bishop Donaghy gave examples in his October 1960 report:

> The Miaoli deanery held its procession [honoring the Blessed Virgin Mary] on the 16th [of October] and all agreed it was the best yet. Several thousand, Catholics and Catechumens, were in the line of march and many more thousands of respectful watchers lined the main streets of the town as the procession wended it's [sic] way through the main arteries. Thirteen gaudily elaborate floats and the lighted candles of the marchers added much color. An unanticipated touch was added as the catechists of the 'separated brethren' passed out leaflets extolling the Protestant doctrine to our Catholic marchers."[106]

By December, Father Capodanno was in the middle of everything. He hired a young man to teach Advent and Christmas hymns to the high school students at the hostels as a means to interest them in the birth of Christ. The young music teacher was studying the faith in preparation for Baptism, and refused payment for his work, but suggested Father might tutor him in English. Father Capodanno wrote his brother Albert,

> So I volunteered to teach him three evenings a week. I'd rather not, since English Classes can be a real time-consumer here. However, I had to do something in return.

---

[105] MFBA, Box: Capodanno Personnel File. Folder: Capodanno, Rev. Vincent R/Documents. Personnel Report, Priests on Mission, August 8, 1961, Bishop Frederick A. Donaghy, MM. Period: July 1, 1960-June 30, 1961.

[106] MFBA, Taiwan Regional Records Reports to General Council 1952-1990, Visitations 1950-1988 Box 7. Folder: Taiwan Records 7/2 Regional Superior's Reports to General Council 1954-1965. Bishop Frederick A. Donaghy, MM, "Monthly Diary of Regional Superior, October, 1960," p. 1r.

Besides, I wanted to make sure that he keeps up on his doctrine studies. His wife is interested, too, but stopped studying since her baby was born a few weeks ago. It would be nice to have them enter the Church. The real strength of a mission is in Catholic families. A husband or a wife, even if his or her children are Baptized, is not nearly as effective as having the whole family Baptized. There is always pagan influence if the whole family is not Catholic.[107]

On February 27, 1961, Father Capodanno's mother died. His family notified him by telegram the next day, offering to bring him home for the funeral. Maryknoll policy prohibited leaving one's mission, even for a parent's funeral. Father immediately offered Mass for the repose of the soul of his beloved mother. [108] He wrote to his family reflecting on the value of Christian hope. To Kathleen he wrote:

> The joys of Heaven are beyond description and the special joys of a mother are surely a magnificent thing. Thru [sic] being in Heaven, a mother may be with each of her children at all times.[109]

He expanded his thoughts a few days later in another letter:

> In many ways, Mary, we have much to be thankful for: it would have been very hard on Mom if she had to be confined to bed, and still not find any real relief from the pain. . . often not even sleep brought relief because the pains in her legs would waken her. Mom would not have enjoyed remaining in bed. Her death was sudden, yes; but her whole life of praying and making so many sacrifices

---

[107] Cap/Staten. Miaoli, December, 1960, Father Vincent R. Capodanno, MM, to Mr. & Mrs. Albert Capodanno.

[108] Cap/Staten. CABLE, Miaoli, March 1, 1961, Father Vincent R. Capodanno, MM, to Albert Capodanno.

[109] AMIL, Box: Correspondence Binder. N.p. March 18, 1961, Father Vincent R. Capodanno, MM, to Kathleen.

prepared her well.

We haven't really lost Mom. Now, in Heaven, she can be with us all and not be away from any of us. How happy that must make Mom. If she was in Jersey with Pauline she wondered about the rest at home. If at home she wondered about Pauline and George and the boys. And, always in the background, no matter whether on the [Staten] Island or in [New] Jersey, she wondered about you, Phil and me. How contented she must be to be able to be with us all at once.

For us, we have the beautiful memories of Mom to sustain us until that time when we all, Mom and Pop and all of us are united permanently in heaven.

The ignorance, fear and hopelessness with which pagans face death must indeed be a terrifying thing to have to go thru [sic] life with. Keep them in your prayers that our work here and in all parts of the world will bring them to a knowlegge [sic] of God and ultimately to eternal happiness, such as we can have for the asking.

I offer Mass each morning for Mom and many other priests on Taiwan have written telling me that they, too, have offered Mass for Mom. Every month a letter goes out from Maryknoll to Maryknollers all over the world telling them of different items of news. Included in this month's letter was notice of Mom's death. This means that Mom will be specifically included in prayers and Masses offered thruout [sic] the world. I have received many, many notes and letters from Maryknoll friends and classmates all over the globe telling me of Masses offered for Mom. Many of my classmates knew Mom from their visits to Maryknoll and some of them from coming home with me when we had a day off. Many of the Catholics here in Miaoli have been praying for Mom, too. I go to a mission in North Miaoli for Sunday Mass and the people there gave me two spiritual bouquets and a stipend for me to say Mass for Mom. I offered that Mass at their mission last Sunday. The boys in the hostel pray for Mom each morning and evening. A Sister I know in Massachusetts wrote to tell me she has her first grade class praying for Mom and all of us, too.[110]

On April 2, 1961, the Chinese press announced the decision by Pope John XXIII to create three new dioceses on Taiwan: The Apostolic Prefecture of Kaohsiung was raised to form the new Diocese of Kaohsiung; the new Diocese of Tainan, with territory detached from the former Apostolic Prefecture of Kaohsiung; and the Diocese of Hsinchu, carved from the Archdiocese of Taipei, which included the districts of Hsinchu, Taoyuan and Miaoli. The announcement included the elevation of Chinese priests as bishops of the new dioceses, and the elevation of Father William Kupfer, MM, as the first Bishop of Hsinchu. [111]

This change affected the Maryknoll missioners. Since the 1949 Communist victory on the mainland, numbers of Chinese priests streamed to Taiwan, often with less than satisfactory results.[112] Now some of them were named bishops, and many of the Maryknoll missioners saw this as problematic. Both Bishop Donaghy and Bishop-designate Kupfer expressed their concerns to their superior. First, the Chinese priests named bishops of the new dioceses were not "native" to Taiwan, and it was generally believed they were uninterested in forming a solid "native" Taiwanese Church. "Moreover, as a rule, they are not welcomed

---

[110] AMIL, Box: Correspondence Binder. Miaoli, March 21, 1961, Father Vincent R. Capodanno, MM, to Mary.

[111] *China Post*, April 2, 1961, *Pontiff Orders Creation of 3 Dioceses in Taiwan*, p. 1.

[112] MFBA, Box: Taiwan Regional Records Correspondence 1960-1968, Box 2. Folder: Taiwan Records 2/1 Regional Superior's Correspondence 1960, Jan-May. Taichung, March 5, 1960, Father William F. Kupfer, MM, to Very Reverend Clarence J. Witte, MM: "These lads [Chinese priests from the mainland] whom we have inherited have been a tremendous disappointment to us."

by the NATIVE people" on Taiwan.[113] Bishop-designate Kupfer knew something about training native sons as priests, since he had purchased a building in 1959 in order to open a new preparatory seminary for local high school boys.[114] The Maryknoll superiors were wary that these decisions would weaken the long-term pastoral efforts and morale of their missioners on Taiwan.

Bishop Donaghy expressed the views of many missionaries on Taiwan, who saw a deeper meaning in Rome's naming of mainland Chinese priests as ordinaries of the new dioceses on Taiwan:

> A) Rome does not share our optimism as to the future stability of Formosa. . . in the event affairs should take a bad turn there native bishops would be able to hold control longer than those from abroad, and B) the new bishops, two of whom have taught for years in Rome, may be able to induce a number of the Chinese Fathers currently living abroad to return to work in their native habitat.[115]

Father Capodanno continued his active local ministry and wrote home offering a thumbnail description of his efforts to extend the Church's influence among the people:

---

[113] MFBA, Taiwan Regional Records Correspondence 1960-1968, Box 2. Folder: Taiwan Records 2/3 Regional Superior's Correspondence 1961. Taichung, April 18, 1961, Bishop-designate William F. Kupfer, MM, to Most Reverend John W. Comber, MM.

[114] MFBA, Taiwan Regional Records Reports to General Council 1952-1990, Visitations 1950-1988, Box 7. Folder: Taiwan Records 7/2 Regional Superior's Reports to General Council 1954-1988. Bishop Frederick A. Donaghy, MM, "Monthly Diary of Regional Superior: Formosa Region, December 1959," p. 1r.

[115] MFBA, Taiwan Regional Records Reports to General Council 1952-1990, Visitations 1950-1988,

Box 7. Folder: Taiwan Records 7/2 Regional Superior's Reports to General Council 1954-1962. Bishop Frederick A. Donaghy, MM, "Monthly Diary of Regional Superior: Formosa Region, April 1961."

Recently, I have increased the number of English classes I teach, not only here at the hostel, but have also taken on three conversation classes at two of the local high schools. Everyone wants to learn Eng[lish]. For us, it is a good way to get to meet many people. Two young boys who have just been coming for English for almost three months just recently asked me to teach them a little bit about the Church. Probably they will never be Baptized, but they are two more who will have some idea of what the Church is and what the real meaning of life is. Maybe sometime in the future they will ask someone for Baptism. In the meantime, they won't have any false notions about what Christ has taught. [116]

By the end of May, it was decided that Father Capodanno should be transferred once again, to Holy Rosary Parish in North Miaoli.[117] Following his annual formal visit with each missioner in his district, Bishop Donaghy recorded the status of Father Capodanno and the reason for moving him. According to Bishop Donaghy, Father Capodanno had made his annual retreat, was in good physical and spiritual health, and was "contented." He was living alone, and his housing and food were "satisfactory." Even though Father Capodanno's spoken and preaching abilities in the Hakka language were good, Bishop Donaghy again judged his written ability to be only "fair," concluding that further formal language studies were needed. Under the category of "Brief estimate of the missioner and his work," Bishop Donaghy wrote that Father Capodanno was:

A good solid priest with a tendency, however, to be a mite harsh in his dealings with the people. It was felt that in his role of Center House Superior and Hostel Director he was

---

[116] AMIL, Box: Correspondence Binder. Miaoli, April 29, 1961, Father Vincent R. Capodanno, MM, to George T. Driscoll.

[117] MFBA, Taiwan Regional Records Correspondence 1960-1968, Box 2. Folder: Taiwan Records 2/3 Regional Superior's Correspondence 1961. Miaoli, June 16, 1961, Circular Letter, p. 2r.

not obtaining enough actual mission experience, so he is now slated to take over, *ad tempus*, as acting pastor of Holy Rosary Parish in North Miaoli when Father Madigan returns home on furlough leave. Gives promise of becoming a fine missioner if he learns to be a little less unbending. [118]

During the summer months, Father Capodanno, as did all Maryknoll missioners in Taiwan, took part in the region-wide parish summer school programs, as coordinated by the Maryknoll superiors of both Taichung and Miaoli. The six-week series of classes was designed to include as many children and adults as possible, offering catechetical classes in the basics of the faith, as well as classes for those preparing for first Communion and Confirmation.[119]

The Father General of Maryknoll, the Most Reverend John W. Comber, MM, visited each Maryknoll mission on Taiwan during the first weeks of November, meeting individually with each Maryknoller.[120] As during his personal interviews with Father Comber in the seminary prior to his ordination to the priesthood, Father Capodanno was quite unambiguous and clear in expressing his opinions to his superior, as the Father General noted:

> CAPODANNO, Father Vincent R.: Assistant in Miaoli. He has done quite well. Definitely of the new school. He doesn't think much of the language course in Hakka.

[118] MFBA, Box: Capodanno Personnel Files. Folder: Capodanno, Rev. Vincent R/Documents. "Personnel Report, Priests on Mission, August 8, 1961. Period: July 1, 1960-June 30, 1961."

[119] MFBA, Taiwan Regional Records Reports to General Council 1952-1990 Visitations 1950-1988, Box 7. Folder: Taiwan Records 7/2 Regional Superior's Reports to General Council 1954-1962. Bishop Frederick A. Donaghy, MM, "Monthly Diary of Regional Superior: Formosa Region, August 1961," p. 1r.

[120] MFBA, Taiwan Regional Records Reports to General Council 1952-1990 Visitations 1950-1988, Box 7. Folder: Taiwan Records 7/2 Regional Superior's Reports to General Council, 1954-1962. Bishop Frederick A. Donaghy, MM, "Monthly Diary of Regional Superior: Formosa Region, November 1961," p. 1r.

Father Donald Sheehan didn't either. Father Hilbert was director, but took no interest in it. Students would probably be better off at Taichung with Hakka teacher. Bishop Donaghy thinks young priests will sort of absorb language.[121]

Under Bishop Donaghy's stewardship, the Miaoli Deanery was adequately staffed, having a good number of priests and religious sisters. The younger priests, however, were transferred frequently. The difficulty was they were "spread rather thinly and furlough leaves and illnesses sometimes make it difficult, if not impossible, to give each parish the attention and follow up it requires."[122] This meant that any plans for further expansion into the more rural areas and smaller towns were hindered, and the younger and healthier priests were called upon to move frequently to temporarily manage parishes whose pastors were ill or on furlough. This was a frustrating reality for some younger missioners eager to invest themselves in mission work.

Once again, Father Capodanno was called upon to move. In May, 1962 he was transferred back to Tunglo, since the pastor, Father Maynard Murphy, MM, was recovering from severe asthma. For a time, Father Capodanno also continued to manage Holy Rosary Parish in Miaoli, until the return of the pastor, Father Madigan, MM, from his furlough. Upon his arrival in Tunglo, he found the number of Catholics to have doubled to 750 persons.[123]

In his annual visit and interview, Bishop Donaghy made

---

[121] MFBA, Taiwan Regional Records Reports to General Council 1952-1990 Visitations 1950-1988, Box 7. Folder: Taiwan Records 7/7 Regional Superior's Visitation Reports 1957-1964. Miaoli, November 1961, Most Reverend John W. Comber, MM, "VISITATION REPORT," p. 3.

[122] MFBA, Taiwan Regional Records Correspondence 1960-1968 Box 2. Folder: Taiwan Records Regional Superior's Correspondence 1961. Miaoli, December 29, 1961, Bishop Frederick A. Donaghy, MM, to Very Reverend John F. Donovan, MM.

[123] AMIL, Box: Correspondence Binder. N.p., June 10, 1962, Father Vincent R. Capodanno, MM, to George T. Driscoll.

this observation of Father Capodanno:

> A fine priestly type he appears interested greatly in the work but innately a perfectionist he finds much in the way of life and customs that irks him more than a little. However, he willingly and gladly undertakes any role assigned him.[124]

As the opening of the Second Vatican Council drew near, many priests around the world looked forward to changes in the methods employed in their pastoral life and local ministry. Some of the younger Maryknoll missioners wanted to do more, but felt restrained by Maryknoll policies, practices and rules judged out-of-date by some of the younger and older priests. Young priests, such as Fathers Capodanno and Sheehan, as well as some of the older, more seasoned priests, thought various Maryknoll policies and practices should be updated, and, as will be seen, expressed themselves respectfully, if forcibly, to their superiors. Father Capodanno had done this while still in the seminary, as described above. Then, he energetically expressed his idea that deacons at Maryknoll should be encouraged to develop a sense of responsibility, instead of being hemmed in by daily rules that discouraged personal initiative in men who would soon be assigned to the foreign missions, and often find themselves alone.

An example of needed practical updating on Taiwan was the matter of the monthly stipend—the *viatique*—given Maryknoll missioners, upon which they were expected to pay all living expenses. The stipend in Taiwan totaled around $65.00 USA per month per priest. For priests living alone in missions, this was insufficient to purchase nourishing, fresh food, which was expensive in the towns, and to operate a rectory and church. The question came to a head in the summer of 1963 when two

---

[124] MFBA, Box: Capodanno Personnel Files. Folder: Capodanno, Rev. Vincent R/Documents. Miaoli, June 27, 1962, Bishop Frederick A. Donaghy, MM: "Personnel Report, Priest on Mission, June 27, 1962, for period: July 1, 1961 to June 30, 1962," p. 1v.

Maryknoll priests from Korea visited Taiwan. Each Maryknoller in Korea received $100.00 USA each month. Once the Maryknoll missionaries on Taiwan heard that, they felt slighted. Bishop Donaghy agreed, and suggested that an increase should be made, at least for those priests living alone in a mission. Even a slight increase in the monthly *viatique* would help improve morale and contribute to the missioners' better health, because they could purchase better food. He continued,

> I write of this matter, and hurriedly, at this time as I feel there is a movement on foot, not general by any means but in enough quarters to make for a bad spirit, to make some sort of an issue on the matter of viatique, or its insufficiency.[125]

Another complaint about outdated Maryknoll rules and practical mission life on Taiwan, was a prohibition against the use of air conditioners in parishes. It was well known that the Maryknoll vicar general to Bishop Donaghy in Taichung and the Maryknoll superior in Hong Kong had air conditioned rooms, yet the priests in mission parishes on Taiwan were not given the same permission or consideration.[126] These seemingly minor complaints led to mistrust and contentious relations between the priests and their superiors. However, there were also serious personality difficulties between the two Maryknoll superiors,

---

[125] MFBA, Taiwan Regional Records Correspondence 1960-1968 Box 2. Folder: Taiwan Records 2/5, Regional Superior's Correspondence 1963. Miaoli, July 30, 1963, Bishop Frederick A. Donaghy, MM, to Most Reverend John W. Comber, MM, p. 2r.

[126] MFBA, Taiwan Regional Records Reports to General Council 1952-1990 Visitations 1950-1988 Box 7. Folder: Taiwan Records 7/7 Regional Superior's Visitation Reports 1957-1964. Hong Kong, July 2, 1964, Very Reverend John F. Donovan, MM, to Bishop Frederick A. Donaghy, MM, p. 1r.

themselves, on Taiwan,[127] as well as among the younger Maryknoll priests and Bishop Donaghy.

In the spring of 1963, because Bishop Kupfer had been named founding bishop of the Diocese of Hsinchu, Bishop Donaghy was instructed by his Maryknoll superiors to move from Miaoli to Taichung, and to live at the Maryknoll Center House. Bishop Kupfer, who had lived in Taichung as the Maryknoll regional superior, protested vehemently against Bishop Donaghy's move, but to no avail. A new regional vicar for Miaoli was needed. Bishop Donaghy personally wanted Father Madigan named, but others wanted another priest, Father Gaiero. The Bishop wrote the Father General:

> However, I now fear that his [Father Madigan's] appointment as Regional Vicar would be interpreted by some as a perpetuation of the old policy, a policy with which not a few reportedly drastically disagree. So under the circumstances, to insure a real esprit de corps in Miaoli, I think it might be well to name Father Gaiero as the Regional Vicar.
>
> Re: Consultors. I agree if you think it advisable to appoint Fr. Faucher as one of the consultors. He is popular with the younger Fathers and they would be sure to look upon his appointment as a much needed injection of young blood in this Region. I also consider him a good missioner who runs a rather taut ship in his own

---

[127] MFBA, Taiwan Regional Records Correspondence 1960-1968 Box 2. Folder: Taiwan Records 2/5 Regional Superior's Correspondence 1963. Numerous letters between Bishop Kupfer and the Father General on this disputed decision and others. Also: MFBA, Taiwan Regional Records Correspondence 1960-1968 Box 2. Folder: Taiwan Records 2/6 Regional Superior's Correspondence 1964. Maryknoll, April 7, 1964, Most Reverend John W. Comber, MM, to Bishop Frederick A. Donaghy, MM. Referring to the anger of Bishop Kupfer concerning various personnel decisions involving Bishop Donaghy, the Father General wrote: "I really think that it would be the best thing to do because of the strained situation that has existed during the past few years. We have to make allowances for personalities."

mission.[128]

Father Capodanno was given another new assignment at this time as the pastor of Saint John the Baptist Parish in Ch'ng An, on the outskirts of Miaoli. It was a small parish with only 543 Catholics, with an average attendance at Sunday Mass of only 140 persons; no one attended daily Mass. Father and one lay catechist were busy teaching classes in Catholic doctrine for 313 Catholic men, women and children, and another 150 attended Baptismal instructions.[129] It was also a very isolated parish, rendered inaccessible by car as a result of storms in 1963.[130]

Bishop Donaghy visited Father Capodanno in the summer of 1963, soon after Father Capodanno arrived in Ch'ng An. He reported that the new pastor's language skills had improved because of his recent language studies while working at the Boys' Hostel. The bishop also noted that Father Capodanno was "contented" in his attitude, but noted also that,

> Father is a perfectionist and for that reason, I believe, finds the life here difficult and this in turn causes him to treat the people with severity. He is a good solid priest but it is difficult to conceive him adopting the rough and ready attitude that certain phases of our

---

[128] MFBA, Taiwan Regional Records Correspondence 1960-1968 Box 2. Folder: Taiwan Records 2/5 Regional Superior's Correspondence 1963. Miaoli, April 20, 1963, Bishop Frederick A. Donaghy, MM, to Most Reverend John W. Comber, MM, pp. 1-2.

[129] MFBA, Taiwan Regional Records, Statistical Reports Taichung 1951-1964; Miaoli 1957-1964, Box 10. Folder: Taiwan Records, 10/5, Statistical Reports, Miaoli 1957-1964, Parish/Dean's Summaries. Bishop Frederick A. Donaghy, MM, "Parish Statistical Report: July 1, 1962-June 30, 1963."

[130] MFBA, Taiwan Regional Records to General Council 1952-1990 Visitations 1950-1988 Box 7. Folder: Taiwan Records 7/7 Regional Superior's Visitation Reports 1957-1964. VISITATION REPORT: Taiwan, June 1964, Very Reverend John F. Donovan, MM, p. 2r.

work demands. [sic][131]

But, Father Capodanno was not "contented." This was not merely because he was transferred frequently, or because of the isolated area to which he had been assigned recently by Bishop Donaghy, nor because he was a perfectionist, as some thought.

Just a few weeks after the bishop's visit, Father Capodanno wrote an extraordinary and long letter to Father John F. Donovan, MM, vicar general of Maryknoll.[132] Father Capodanno and other Maryknoll priests of the region questioned Bishop Donaghy's recent appointment of a temporary superior necessitated by the bishop's attending the opening of the second session of the Second Vatican Council. Bishop Donaghy's choice was not agreeable to many of the younger Maryknoll priests, hence his letter. The issue was confusing because it dealt with the delegated authority of Bishop Donaghy as regional superior of the Maryknoll missioners, granted him by the Father General of Maryknoll, and his delegated authority as rural dean of all parishes in Miaoli, which faculties were granted him by Archbishop Petrus Pao-Zin Tou, the Ordinary of the Archdiocese of Taipei. Father Capodanno insisted that Bishop Donaghy's decision was contrary to the Maryknoll Constitutions.

The Father General responded to Father Capodanno on September 6, 1963, writing,

> I know that you make your suggestions in good spirit and we want you to be free to do so. The administration of the [Maryknoll] Society and its members is something completely distinct from the administration of the [local]

---

[131] MFBA, Box: Capodanno Personnel Files; Folder: Capodanno, Rev. Vincent R/Documents. Bishop Frederick A. Donaghy, MM: "Personnel Report, Priests on Mission, August 1, for the period July 1, 1962 to June 30, 1963," p. 1v.

[132] MFBA, Box: Capodanno Personnel Files. Folder: Capodanno, Rev. Vincent R/Documents. "Tai an Ching an Miaoli," August 23, 1963, Father Vincent R. Capodanno, MM, to Very Reverend John F. Donovan, MM. This is an eight-page typed letter.

Diocese or any ecclesiastical divisions of the Diocese.[133]

While the Miaoli Archdiocesan Deanery and the Maryknoll Region were canonically distinct entities, in reality, Bishop Donaghy administered both as if he were the ordinary instead of a mere vicar. There had been other complaints about Bishop Donaghy, so that the Father General and his general council had some questions during the winter of 1964 about aspects of Bishop Donaghy's administration, and about the developing tensions between Bishop Donaghy and Bishop Kupfer. Answering a letter from the Father General of Maryknoll, which informed him that three priests would be sent to Bishop Kupfer and only one to his own region during the next months, Bishop Donaghy defended his administration:

> With you I sincerely hope that this arrangement may tend to do away with any tension existing here at present. I am not a little chagrined that there is tension as I have ever tried to act objectively in my role as Regional Superior. In the distribution both of funds and personnel I have never acted except in consort with my Consultors; nor have I ever employed undue pressure or argument to foist my view on them. This change in the appointments may lead to certain repercussions, assuredly it will lead to much talk, but such I can readily sustain if, as is hoped, it will lead to smoother relationships.[134]

Father Capodanno continued his work in his small parish, and the parish grew under his leadership, as seen in the parish report of the summer of 1964: the number of Catholics rose to 568 persons, with an increase in catechumens and Catholics

---

[133] MFBA, Box: Capodanno Personnel Files. Folder: Capodanno, Rev. Vincent R/Documents. Maryknoll, September 6, 1963, Bishop John W. Comber, MM, to Father Vincent R. Capodanno, MM.

[134] MFBA, Taiwan Regional Records Correspondence 1960-1968 Box 2. Folder: Taiwan Records 2/6 Regional Superior's Correspondence 1964. Miaoli, April 26, 1964, Bishop Frederick A. Donaghy, MM, to Most Reverend John W. Comber, MM, p. 1r.

studying Catholic doctrine. Father Capodanno began innovations that would become commonplace around the world with the changes of the Second Vatican Council: "Three men and three women volunteer Catechists who act as representatives of the Church, each in his or her own area, and attempt to intensify Catholic activities."[135]

The vicar general of Maryknoll, Very Reverend John F. Donovan, MM, arrived in Taipei on May 28, 1964 to begin his visitation of all the Maryknoll missions in Hong Kong and on Taiwan. In early June he visited Ch'ng An, and interviewed Father Capodanno, [136] and noted:

> He had many complaints. He obviously is not happy here. He complained of the language study set-up—hopeless. He said the present regional superior was forced on them by the [Maryknoll] Center. Council members said Bishop Donaghy would be appointed before second ballot was in. Bishop Donaghy is more interested in Miaoli mission than in the Region—men have no recourse.

As Father Donovan discovered, Father Capodanno was not the only Maryknoll missioner who was unhappy, or who had complaints about Bishop Donaghy's administration as Regional Superior of the Maryknoll missions. The complaints were that the language school was terrible; Bishop Donaghy never consulted with his Consultors about the opening of new parishes, convents or personnel changes; ordinary priests had no voice in formulating the policy of the region; Bishop Donaghy's choice as his replacement in Miaoli, Father McCabe,

---

[135] MFBA, Box 10: Taiwan Regional Records. Statistical Reports Taichung 1951-1964, Miaoli 1953-1969; Folder: Taiwan Records 10/10, Statistical Reports. Miaoli Parishes 1958-1969. "Parish Statistical Report: July 1, 1963 to June 30, 1964."

[136] MFBA, Taiwan Regional Records Reports to General Council 1952-1990 Visitations 1950-1988, Box 7. Folder: Taiwan Records 7/7 Regional Superior's Visitation Reports 1957-1964. Taiwan, June 1964, Very Reverend John F. Donovan, MM, "VISITATION REPORT," p. 2r.

berated the priests, especially when asked for living allowances; and there was a general sense that the election of Bishop Donaghy as superior was rigged.[137]

Two priests expressed satisfaction with the bishop. Both were "Old China Hands" who had worked as missionaries on the mainland until expelled by the Communist government. One was Father Henry Madigan, MM. The other was Father Maynard Murphy, MM, former pastor of Father Capodanno, who stated that the problems were caused by the younger fathers who "must have something to gripe about."[138]

Another Maryknoll missionary on Taiwan at the time was Father J. Donald McGinnis, MM, who described the tension between the "Old China Hands" and the younger missionaries who had not served on the mainland, among whom was Father Capodanno:

> Father Capodanno was a gentleman, always well groomed, very neat, not what might be called a 'rough and tumble' fellow. Sometimes I felt that the older men, those who had come from mainland China had the opinion of Father Capodanno that he was not, did not have the 'right stuff.' He certainly showed later that he had guts. [139]

After the completion of his visitation of Taiwan, Father Donovan went on to visit and evaluate Maryknoll's work in Hong

---

[137] MFBA, Taiwan Regional Records Reports to General Council 1952-1990 Visitations 1950-1988, Box 7. Folder: Taiwan Records 7/7 Regional Superior's Visitation Reports 1957-1964. Taiwan, June 1964, Very Reverend John F. Donovan, MM, "VISITATION REPORT," p. 1r. Other Maryknoll priests who lodged complaints were, Fathers Elmer Wurth, Donald McGinnis, Henry Madigan, and Brendan O'Connell.

[138] MFBA, Taiwan Regional Records Reports to General Council 1952-1990 Visitations 1950-1988, Box 7. Folder: Taiwan Records 7/7 Regional Superior's Visitation Reports 1957-1964. Taiwan, June 1964, Very Reverend John F. Donovan, MM, "Visitation Report," p. 1r.

[139] AMIL, Box: Capodanno Personal Testimonies. Ossining, NY, March 28, 2014, Father J. Donald McGinnis, MM, to Monsignor Stephen M. DiGiovanni.

Kong. There, he received a response from the Father General to his reports about Taiwan. In his letter, Bishop Comber wrote about Bishop Donaghy:

> Certainly it is Bishop Donaghy who suggested to [Arch] Bishop Tou the man to appoint as Dean while he is away [at Vatican II], but I do not know what we can do about it. We shall have to take some time to work it out. I am sure that the men there probably think that Father Faucher received an overwhelming number of votes for Regional Superior, and that we disregarded them. As you know, he received no more than Bishop Donaghy.[140]

Father Donovan replied, describing the divisions among the Maryknoll priests and their local superior:

> At one point I thought the feeling against Bishop Donaghy was quite general, however as I moved about I found that the majority of the men went along with the appointment [as Regional Superior]. Those who opposed the reappointment of Bishop Donaghy certainly have strong feelings about it and of course those are the voices that make the most noise.
>
> There is no question about it there is a deep feeling on the part of Bishop Kupfer and Father McCabe against Bishop Donaghy. McCabe can control his feelings in Bishop Donaghy's presence, but apparently Bishop Kupfer finds it impossible and this fact is recognized throughout the Region.[141]

---

[140] MFBA, Taiwan Regional Records Reports to General Council 1952-1990 Visitations 1950-1988 Box 7. Folder: Taiwan Records 7/7 Regional Superior's Visitation Reports 1957-1964. Maryknoll, June 15, 1964, Most Reverend John W. Comber, MM, to Very Reverend John F. Donovan, MM, p. 1r.

[141] MFBA, Taiwan Regional Records Reports to General Council 1952-1990 Visitations 1950-1988 Box 7. Folder: Taiwan Records 7/7 Regional Superior's Visitation Reports 1957-1964. Hong Kong June 25, 1964, Very Reverend John F. Donovan, MM, to Most Reverend John W. Comber, MM, pp. 1r-2r.

Having completed his first six-year term in Taiwan, Father Capodanno took advantage of the traditional six-month furlough offered Maryknoll missioners. Leaving his mission on August 17th, he traveled to Japan to meet Father Richard Murto, MM, his classmate from Maryknoll, who was also beginning his furlough, with whom he visited the Holy Land.[142] Father Capodanno then traveled to England, stayed three days, and then continued on to the United States, arriving in October.[143] He stayed with his sister Pauline and her family in Kearny, New Jersey, visited friends and family, and helped at the local parish by offering Masses.

---

[142] Mode, *The Grunt Padre*, p. 49.

[143] MFBA, Box: Capodanno Personnel Files; Folder: Capodanno, Rev. Vincent R/Documents. Kearney, N.J., January 30, 1965, Father Vincent R. Capodanno, MM, to Mrs. Patrick O'Connell.

Chapter IV

Hong Kong and Hawaii

After his visit home, Father Capodanno returned to Taiwan on Monday, March 8, 1965. In a letter to friends, Father Capodanno told them "I had such a perfect time I have been telling everyone here that my furlough was the best in the history of Maryknoll."[144] The very day he returned, Father Capodanno was instructed to report to Bishop Donaghy, immediately, and was informed of his new assignment to Hong Kong to teach in the Maryknoll Fathers School. "I was the only free person around so all factors rolled into one fact: I go to Hong Kong," he reported to his family.[145] He was unsure if this would be a temporary or permanent reassignment. But it was to be permanent, as Bishop Donaghy wrote Father William Collins, MM, in a letter marked "P.C.," personal and confidential. [146]

Bishop Donaghy confirmed the need for a priest in Hong Kong. Several Maryknoll priests there were due to take their furloughs, while others were being transferred to new assignments, and others were in ill health.[147] During the Maryknoll annual retreat in Hong Kong, Bishop Donaghy had spoken of his idea to transfer Father Capodanno with Father McLoughlin, who served as vicar general for Hong Kong.[148] The

---

[144] AMIL, Box: Correspondence Binder. Miaoli, March 14, 1965, Father Vincent R. Capodanno, MM, to Dr. & Mrs. George Costa.

[145] AMIL, Ibid.

[146] MFBA, Taiwan Regional Records Correspondence 1960-1968 Box 2. Folder: Taiwan Records 2/7 Regional Superior's Correspondence 1965. Miaoli, April 4, 1965, Bishop Frederick A. Donaghy, MM, to Very Reverend William Collins, MM.

[147] MFBA, Taiwan Regional Records Correspondence 1960-1968 Box 2. Folder: Taiwan Records 2/6 Regional "Superior's Correspondence 1964. Miaoli, March 21, 1964, Bishop Frederick A. Donaghy, MM, to Most Reverend John W. Comber, MM, p. 1r.

[148] MFBA, Taiwan Regional Records Correspondence 1960-1968 Box 2. Folder: Taiwan Records 2/7 Regional Superior's Correspondence 1965. Miaoli, July 18, 1965, Bishop Frederick A. Donaghy, MM, to Most Reverend John W. Comber, MM, p. 1r.

bishop claimed that Father Capodanno's transfer became urgent with the unexpected illness of Father Peter Reilly, MM. He was the supervisor of the Maryknoll Fathers' School, liaison with the Crown Colony Department of Education for all Maryknoll schools, and pastor of a thriving parish in Kuntong. He was seriously overweight, and his extremely high blood pressure brought about a sudden collapse and unexpected illness. This was one of the stated reasons for the urgency of transferring Father Capodanno immediately upon his return from his furlough.[149]

The formal announcement was made by Bishop Donaghy in his circular letter to all Maryknollers in the region on March 27, 1965:

> On the 21st of this month Father Capodanno left with the well wishes of all, to assume his new role in the Maryknoll Fathers' School in Hongkong. [sic] However, Father's efforts will not be limited merely to teaching in the classroom as there is no dearth of outlet for missionary zeal in this work. Illness of Father Reilly together with pending furloughs and personnel changes created a real sense of urgency in this assignment.[150]

There was a real need for additional Maryknoll priests in Hong Kong. The mass arrival of refugees from mainland China and other parts of Asia was forcing the local Crown colonial government to construct large tenement buildings to house them. During Father Donovan's 1964 visitation, he wrote to the Father General suggesting an addition to their high school that would allow Maryknoll to open a new parish mission in

[149] MFBA, Taiwan Regional Records Reports to General Council 1952-1990 Visitations 1950-1988 Box 7. Folder: Taiwan Records 7/3 Regional Superior's Reports to General Council 1963-1968. Bishop Frederick A. Donaghy, MM: "Monthly Diary of Regional Superior, February & March 1965," p. 1r-2r.

[150] MFBA, Taiwan Regional Records Correspondence 1960-1968 Box 2. Folder: Taiwan Records 2/7 Regional Superior's Correspondence 1965. Miaoli, March 27, 1965, Circular Letter.

conjunction with the high school, close by the new tenements. He wrote:

> As you know, wherever we establish a school-parish type of mission in these Hong Kong resettlement areas within three or four years we have a parish of four or five thousand Catholics. To me it seems like an extraordinary opportunity. The people are all within a few minutes walk of the church and school and the priests and catechists can reach them easily, provided they don't mind climbing stairs.[151]

In his monthly regional superior's report, Bishop Donaghy described Father Capodanno's response to his transfer:

> He expressed a desire to remain in Miaoli but accepted the assignment in, I believe, good part when I explained the urgent need for someone with experience in Hongkong [sic] forthwith. He is a good solid priest and will, I am confident, accomplish more effective work in this field. However, his efforts will not be confined entirely to teaching; he will be given an opportunity to acquire Cantonese and will have no dearth of outlet for his missionary zeal.[152]

That was not entirely accurate. For, while Father Capodanno had accepted the Bishop's assignment to Hong Kong as an obedient missioner, he was uneasy about being removed from parish mission work on Taiwan. For he had been trained specifically for mission work on Taiwan and had struggled to learn the Hakka language. Now, he was to be removed from Taiwan to teach

---

[151] MFBA, Taiwan Regional Records Reports to General Council 1952-1990 Visitations 1950-1988 Box 7. Folder: Taiwan Records 7/7 Regional Superior's Visitation Reports 1957-1964. Davao City, Philippines, July 7, 1964, Very Reverend John F. Donovan, MM, to Most Reverend John W. Comber, MM, p. 2r.

[152] MFBA, Taiwan Regional Records to General Council 1952-1990 Visitations 1950-1988 Box 7. Folder: Taiwan Records 7/3 Regional Superior's Reports to General Council 1963-1968. Bishop Frederick A. Donaghy, MM, "Monthly Diary of Regional Superior, February & March 1965," p. 1r.

English in a high school in Hong Kong, and told to learn yet another Chinese dialect. After meeting with Bishop Donaghy, Father Capodanno went to see a fellow missionary, Father J. Donald McGinnis, MM, then the pastor of the Maryknoll parish in Tahu. Father McGinnis recalled the visit:

> Father Vincent Capodanno visited me in my parish in Tahu, Taiwan. He was extremely upset. He said that he had just been told by the Maryknoll Regional Superior and the Miaoli County Deanery that he was to be assigned to Hong Kong. This came as a shock to Father Capodanno.[153]

Father McGinnis continued, providing some of the reasons why Father Capodanno was upset by his sudden reassignment by Bishop Donaghy to Hong Kong:

> The Maryknollers working in Miaoli spoke Hakka, a Chinese dialect, whereas Maryknollers in Hong Kong spoke Cantonese (another Chinese dialect). I thought at first that Father Peter Reilly had requested a priest from Miaoli to teach English since he was both a good friend of Bishop Donaghy and needed an English teacher because he was in charge of the Maryknoll Fathers High School in Hong Kong. I discovered that Father Reilly had not requested an English teacher. Father Reilly was completely surprised when Father Capodanno arrived.[154]

It became obvious that, while there was a real pastoral need for more Maryknoll priests in Hong Kong to minister among the thousands of arriving immigrants fleeing mainland China, there was no real need for Father Capodanno to teach English in the high school. Father McGinnis then suggested to Father Capodanno that he return "to ask Bishop Donaghy to reconsider because it was his [Father Capodanno's] earnest wish to

---

[153] AMIL, Box: Capodanno, Maryknoll. Ossining, March 28, 2014, Father J. Donald McGinnis, MM, to Monsignor Stephen M. DiGiovanni.

[154] AMIL, Ibid.

continue his work in Miaoli."

The situation became tense, as Bishop Donaghy related to the Father General, three months later. But the bishop was less than truthful, for it was the bishop, not Father Capodanno, who wanted the meeting, summoning the priest on the day he returned from his vacation to the United States:

On my return from Hongkong [sic], Father Capodanno, shortly back from leave, called asking if he might visit me that evening. At the time of the call Father Faucher happened to be with me but left before Father Capodanno's arrival. I had explained the matter to Father Faucher and he considered the assignment [to Hong Kong], as an assignment, 'a perfect one' but added that he feared 'repercussions'. On Father Capodanno's arrival I explained the urgent need in Hongkong [sic] and though he did state a preference to remain in Miaoli, he accepted the assignment. He told me he knew and admired Mrs. Tong, principal of the School, having met her some years ago in the States, and added that he already had an 'in' with here [sic] and her son Robert is his dentist in Hongkong [sic]. The talk took place on Saturday evening and as he was leaving he informed me that he would phone Father Quirk on the morrow to have a reservation made for Thursday's flight from Taipei to Hongkong [sic]. Frankly, I concluded the assignment appealed to him and was pleased that it did.

However, later the same evening from the Tahu mission he attempted, without success, to reach Father Faucher by telephone. Whether within an hour or two after leaving here he had second thoughts or had received advice, I do not know.

The following morning, Sunday, he sought me out at the Tunglo mission where I was assisting Father Maynard Murphy, to talk the matter over. Following a discussion of half an hour or more, during which he expressed a strong desire to remain here and from my part I stressed the sense of urgency in Hongkong [sic], he again accepted the assignment and at the end of the week set out from Taipei. Then followed the correspondence which I enclose.[155]

The Bishop continued, admitting for the first time that some Maryknoll priests thought that Father Capodanno was not being treated fairly by Bishop Donaghy, and that there were other factors involved in Father Capodanno's "change of heart":

> In some quarters, here, particularly I believe, amongst the younger men, there is a feeling that he has been 'railroaded' but I can honestly, and happily, state that this is not the case. In the assignment, which was by no means a spur of the moment decision, I thought only of the work and of him. . . in that order. He is a good priest but temperamentally unsuited to deal with the type of people met with in our work here. In Hongkong [sic] however, and more particularly in the Maryknoll Fathers' School, he would meet and associate with those more in line with his natural temperament. I am thoroughly convinced he could accomplish much there if he set his mind to it.

> If he wishes to continue on in Hongkong [sic] I would be happy to have him there. However, I personally feel, and my consultors share the view, that it would be a mistake to have him return to Taiwan as there certainly then would be 'repercussions' of a serious nature.

Other factors that may have played a part in Bishop Donaghy's decisions about Father Capodanno should be kept in mind, as well. Father Capodanno had formally protested in

---

[155] MFBA, Taiwan Regional Records Correspondence 1960-1968 Box 2. Folder: Taiwan Records 2/7 Regional Superior's Correspondence 1965. Miaoli, July 18, 1965, Bishop Frederick A. Donaghy, MM, to Most Reverend John W. Comber, MM, pp.2r-3r.

writing to the Father General about Bishop Donaghy's decision concerning his replacement in Miaoli during his absence at the Vatican Council. He also aired his views about Bishop Donaghy during the visitation of Father Donovan, M.M. These two formal protests, combined with the "preferential treatment" alleged to have been given by Maryknoll superiors to missioners of Irish or German background, may also have contributed to Bishop Donaghy's removal of Father Capodanno from Taiwan. [156]

Another Maryknoll missioner, Father Elmer P. Wurth, MM, who was on Taiwan at the time and knew Father Capodanno, described his experience:

> He [Father Capodanno] was a good and zealous missioner in the mts. [mountains] of Taiwan near me. He took part in all the [Maryknoll] gatherings of our deanery, but there was nothing that stood out in his ministry. He was thorough in every aspect of mission, but did not give the impression that he was exceptional. I wrote what I did principally because the way he [Fr. Capodanno] humbly responded to the way the bishop [Bishop Donaghy] made life difficult for him. He seemed to lose much when the bishop unexpectedly punished him for disagreeing with him when the bishop acted contrary to our [Maryknoll] Constitutions [Regarding Bishop Donaghy's replacement during the Second Vatican Council]. He [Bishop Donaghy] moved him [Father Capodanno] from being a happy and energetic mt. missioner to teaching English in Hong Kong where he had to learn a completely new Chinese language to find fulfillment in his ministry. I know he was deeply hurt by the way he was treated and pretty much went into a shell. He had a few Maryknoll friends, but no longer participated enthusiastically in our bigger Maryknoll gatherings or in the diocesan structure of meetings, etc. he seemed to be biding his time until he could get out

---

[156] The author's conversation with a retired Maryknoll missionary who had worked with Father Capodanno on Taiwan. He preferred to remain anonymous.

from under a superior who had so deflated his enthusiasm. That opportunity came when he was accepted as a military chaplain. The rest is what changed him from a happy missioner to a deeply hurt missioner to a hero. He proved to the bishop that he was tough enough for any assignment. The way he handled the difficult situation is noteworthy. He did not ask for arbitration, but simply moved on with his life.[157]

The divisions among the Maryknoll missionaries were also in play in Bishop Donaghy's decision, as outlined by Father James P. Nieckarz, MM, who arrived in Taiwan in 1966, a few months after Father Capodanno's entry into the military. He recalled the problems among the Maryknoll priests on Taiwan:

> I was in the Taichung diocese under Bishop William Kupfer, MM. As in Miaoli (where Father Capodanno had been assigned), the majority of the missioners there were older—'Old China Hands', who had served in China until they were expelled in 1950 + moved to Hong Kong. The newer younger priests were relatively few. But in Taichung, although we had different theological + missiological ideas, + ideas that were freely expressed at Society meetings, personnel morale was good. We respected each other + got along socially quite well. We were a larger + more diverse diocese than the Miaoli area, a Prelature [sic] under Bishop Donaghy, MM.
>
> In my second year I traveled to Miaoli. One of the main reasons I went, was to find out why Father Capodanno had been so suddenly transferred to Hong Kong. I had heard conflicting reasons + wanted to try to clarify the situation. I still considered him a role model + the younger members of the Region were also surprised + some were rather upset about his abrupt departure from

[157] AMIL, Box: Capodanno Personal Testimonies. Kalida, Ohio, March 29, 2014, Father Elmer P. Wurth, MM, to Monsignor Stephen M. DiGiovanni.

Taiwan, R.O.C. [Republic of China].

I was very happy though that I had been assigned to Taichung. Father Vincent had asked at one point to be transferred to Taichung but was transferred to Hong Kong instead. The younger members [of Maryknoll] in Miaoli were few (5 or 6) and seemed to be marginalized + when Father Vincent arrived, there were even fewer who had not served in China. A great divide seemed to exist between the two groups which did not exist in Taichung. Father Vincent as a young, Italian-American, who was somewhat reserved + proper in his manner + attire, who had a piety + spirituality that stood out in a way that made some members 'uncomfortable', led to the conclusion that he didn't quite 'fit in'. He did struggle with the language, but so did most of the other members of the Region.

Based on what I have learned about Father Vincent, I would say he suffered a lot of emotional + psychological distress in both Taiwan + Hong Kong because he was made to feel rather unwelcomed or, as some have said, he simply did not 'fit in', in the opinion of the local 'establishment.' [158]

Father Capodanno obeyed Bishop Donaghy, traveled to Hong Kong, began teaching English in the Maryknoll high school, and studied Cantonese. Once there, however, he became convinced that he was not needed in High School work. In his letter of April 1, 1965, Father Capodanno offered a compromise, asking Bishop Donaghy if he would transfer him to Taichung after one year of language courses in Hong Kong.[159] The bishop refused, replying on April 6th that the assignment to teach high

---

[158] AMIL, Box: Capodanno, Maryknoll. Staten Island, July 12, 2006, Father James P. Nieckarz, MM, to Mary Preece.

[159] MFBA, Taiwan Regional Correspondence 1960-1968 Box 2. Folder: Taiwan Records 7/2 Regional Superior's Correspondence 1965. Hong Kong, April 1, 1965, Father Vincent R. Capodanno, MM, to Bishop Frederick A. Donaghy, MM.

school and study Cantonese in Hong Kong remained unchanged.[160] On April 9th, Father Capodanno again wrote Bishop Donaghy:

> I request to be relieved of all duties, teaching and/or parochial, in order to be able to devote full time to the study of language, in accordance with [Maryknoll] Constitutions Paragraph #194. I further request that this period of language study be for me two years as is the presently recommended procedure for Maryknoll in general and as is the actual practice in several Maryknoll Regions.[161]

Bishop Donaghy again denied the request, answering on April 21st:

> In response to your letter of April the 9th, due to the sense of urgency we would like to have you continue teaching in the Maryknoll Fathers' School and postpone, at least for the time being, an intensive course of language study such as you have suggested.
>
> The transition from Hakka to Cantonese you will find much less difficult than it might first appear and I am sure Father McLoughlin will supply you a teacher and the required books.[162]

In his usual Easter form letter to family and friends, Father Capodanno gave no hint that there were problems or that he was dissatisfied. He described the school and the courses he was teaching, and wrote about Hong Kong and the large number of refugees:

[160] MFBA, Ibid., Miaoli, April 6, 1965, Bishop Frederick A. Donaghy, MM, to Reverend Vincent R. Capodanno, MM.

[161] MFBA, Ibid., Hong Kong, April 9, 1965, Father Vincent R. Capodanno, MM, to Bishop Frederick A. Donaghy, MM.

[162] MFBA, Taiwan Regional Correspondence 1960-1968 Box 2. Folder: Taiwan Records 2/7 Regional Superior's Correspondence 1965. Miaoli, April 21, 1965, Bishop Frederick A. Donaghy, MM, to Father Vincent R. Capodanno, MM.

Maryknoll Fathers' High School is in the midst of one of these refugee areas and its fifteen hundred students are children of refugees. Though these refugees have lost their homeland, your prayers will help them find God. [163]

But there were problems, and these were highlighted in the brief report made to the Maryknoll superiors by Doctor John Carey-Hughes following the physical examination of Father Capodanno in Hong Kong soon after Easter:

> The above was seen by me today and previously by Dr. Park a month ago.
>
> He gives a history of loss of appetite, weight loss of 10 lbs., sleeping badly and increasing nervousness for the past month.
>
> He also has a mild blepharitis associated with a patch of eczema on the left ear and some angular stomatitis.
>
> He has been taking tranquilizers prescribed by Dr. Park on and off for the last month.
>
> I consider his condition to be Anxiety State associated with some neuro-dermatitis due to frustration and problems associated with his present assignment and I feel that his best interest, if not that of the Order too, would be served by a re-assignment of his position. [164]

On May 14th, Bishop Donaghy wrote Father Capodanno granting permission that he enroll in a one year course of Cantonese study at the New Asia College, while insisting that he

---

[163] CAP/Staten, Hong Kong, Easter 1965, Father Vincent Capodanno, MM, to Mr. & Mrs. A. Ishill.

[164] MFBA, Box: Capodanno Personnel files. Folder: Capodanno, Rev. Vincent R/Documents. Hong Kong, April 26, 1965, Dr. John Carey-Hughes "To whom it may concern."

continue teaching at the Maryknoll Fathers' School.[165]

Father Capodanno answered on May 18th. He suggested to the bishop that, since there were other new Maryknoll priests arriving,

> It would seem that one more of these men could be assigned to Hong Kong to begin his mission career in circumstances and for a work that are completely different from the circumstances and work in which I acquired six years experience on Taiwan.
>
> I cannot sit by and watch as that period of time is written off as a total loss. Those six years can be at least salvaged partially by arranging for the use of the experience acquired during them. I therefore ask once more to be sent to Taichung.[166]

He received no response. Twice Father Capodanno telephoned Bishop Donaghy from Hong Kong requesting a written answer to his letter of May 18th, and twice he "was told that it was the unanimous opinion of the Regional Consultors that his assignment to Hongkong [sic] stand unchanged."[167]

On June 3, 1965, Father Capodanno wrote the Father General, requesting to be transferred from the Taiwan-Hong Kong Region and reassigned to another Maryknoll mission region. He cited ill health as the reason for his request, and enclosed the above quoted medical report from Doctor John

---

[165] MFBA, Taiwan Regional Records Correspondence 1960-1968 Box 2. Folder: Taiwan Records 2/7 Regional Superior's Correspondence 1965. Miaoli, May 14, 1965, Bishop Frederick A. Donaghy, MM, to Father Vincent R. Capodanno, MM.

[166] MFBA, Ibid., Hong Kong, May 18, 1965, Father Vincent R. Capodanno, MM, to Bishop Frederick A. Donaghy, MM.

[167] MFBA, Taiwan Regional Records Correspondence 1960-1968 Box 2. Folder: Taiwan Records 2/7 Regional Superior's Correspondence 1965. N.p. July 10, 1965 Bishop Frederick A. Donaghy, MM, to Bishop John W. Comber, MM.

Carey-Hughes. [168] The Father General answered him on June 8th, stating that he would place Father Capodanno's request before the General Council and that he had contacted Father McLoughlin, local superior in Hong Kong. He wrote,

> We don't want to take you from the Taiwan Region if it is at all possible for you to work there. You have studied the language there and you have the ability to succeed as a good missioner. [169]

The Father General encouraged the younger missioner to speak with Father McLoughlin, and continued,

> The doctor's letter seems to indicate that you have a nervous condition. This is something that someone might get in any place in the world and could be of a passing nature. You don't want to make a decision that affects your entire career too quickly. At the same time, I want to emphasize that we wish to help you in every way possible.

The Father General wrote to Father McLoughlin the same day, informing him that Father Capodanno requested to leave the Hong Kong-Taiwan Region:

> There probably is not much we can do about it. We will probably transfer him to the Philippine Region but I think that you should have a talk with him first and see what is on his mind. He has a good knowledge of the Hakka language, he has been prepared for this Region and we

[168] MFBA, Box: Capodanno Personnel Files. Folder: Capodanno, Vincent R/Documents. Kowloon, Hong Kong, June 3, 1965, Father Vincent R. Capodanno, MM, to Bishop John W. Comber, MM.

[169] MFBA, Box: Capodanno Personnel File. Folder: Capodanno, Rev. Vincent R/Documents. Maryknoll, n.p. June 8, 1965, Bishop John W. Comber, MM, to Father Vincent R. Capodanno, MM.

would like to keep him in that Region if at all possible.[170]

On June 9th, the Father General wrote Bishop Donaghy, informing the bishop of his instructions to Father McLoughlin to meet with Father Capodanno. He then made it clear: "We hate to see Father Capodanno leave the Hong Kong-Taiwan area since he has been trained for the mission there. I told Father McLoughlin, as you can see from the letter, to talk with him. It may be a sudden impulse of Father Capodanno."[171]

Father McLoughlin met with Father Capodanno on June 27th, as Bishop Donaghy reported to the Father General:

> This morning I received the following letter from Father McLoughlin:

>> 'After several talks with our friend, I have been unable to determine what is on his mind—as per instructions of Father General,—except that he wishes out of the Taiwan Hongkong [sic] Region. [I] Told him to think it over again for a few days, but he seems determined. If the General wrote and tried persuading him, Vinnie might just be resigned and stay here. At present, he is doing a good job teaching at the MK Fathers School; is liked, and takes a great interest in the youngsters.'[172]

Bishop Donaghy ended his letter, "It might be, as Father Mcloughlin suggests, if you write to him he can be persuaded to continue on in Hongkong [sic]. I repeat, I am thoroughly

---

[170] MFBA, Box: Capodanno Personnel File. Folder: Capodanno, Rev. Vincent R/Documents. Maryknoll, June 8, 1965, Bishop John W. Comber, MM, to Father John M. McLoughlin, MM.

[171] MFBA, Taiwan Regional Records Correspondence 1960-1968 Box 2. Folder: Taiwan Records 2/7 Regional Superior's Correspondence 1965. Maryknoll, June 9, 1965, Bishop John W. Comber, MM, to Bishop Frederick A. Donaghy, MM.

[172] MFBA, Taiwan Regional Records Correspondence 1960-1968 Box. Folder: Taiwan Records Regional Superior's Correspondence 1965. Miaoli, June 27, 1965, Bishop Frederick A. Donaghy, MM, to Bishop John W. Comber, MM.

convinced he is capable of doing a very good job in school work there."

The Father General wrote Father Capodanno on July 8th, as suggested by Bishop Donaghy and Father McLoughlin, encouraging him not to make rash judgments, and to try the Hong Kong assignment for one year. "You can be assured that we want to help you as you are one of our missioners with the ability to do a lot for the Church."[173]

But there was no written response from Father Capodanno. While his superiors awaited word from him, Father Capodanno was investigating the possibility of applying to the United States Navy as a chaplain. He felt his search for information should be completed as quickly as possible before he answered the Father General's letters with any decision. He wanted to be sure he was suitable for acceptance by the Navy. His first doubt was that he might not pass a physical examination. In light of his earlier examination which diagnosed a nervous malady, the possibility that he might be judged ineligible for military service appeared real. Once the question about his physical suitability for military service was answered, as he wrote the Bureau of Naval Personnel, "I felt bound in justice and courtesy to inform my superiors here in Hong Kong of my intention before I was included in the teaching schedule" at the Maryknoll School.[174] Seeking information about the military, he decided to speak with the Marine Liaison Officer at the American consulate in Hong Kong, to ascertain what would be the first practical steps possible to enlist in the United States military while he was in a foreign land.[175]

---

[173] MFBA, Box: Capodanno Personnel Files. Folder: Capodanno, Rev. Vincent R/Documents. Maryknoll, July 8, 1965, Bishop John W. Comber, MM, to Father Vincent R. Capodanno, MM.

[174] AMIL, Box: Correspondence Binder. Kowloon, Hong Kong, August 18, 1965, Father Vincent R. Capodanno, MM, to Lieutenant. Commander Carl A. Auel.

[175] AMIL, Box: Correspondence Binder. Kowloon, Hong Kong, August 18, 1965, Father Vincent R. Capodanno, MM, to Bishop John W. Comber, MM.

For years, Father Capodanno had worked during his vacations in Hong Kong at the Maryknoll Seamen's Wharf, opened to help United States military personnel. He also had offered Masses on United States Navy vessels in the harbor. His decision to enter the Navy and to serve as a chaplain to the United States Marines may have been influenced by this experience, and by the fact that his brother, James, had served as a Marine during World War II. Also, during his first parish assignment on Taiwan, he came into contact with United States Navy and Marine personnel who were the backbone of the American and Maryknoll emergency response following the devastating floods and landslides during the late summer of 1959. So, it was understandable that he consider the Navy and Marines, and that he call upon his American military contacts in the United States Navy and at the United States consulate in Hong Kong, to arrange for a physical examination by a military doctor. He succeeded, and was examined on board the American Battleship *Iwo Jima* on July 13th. [176] He passed the examination, and the doctor's final written comment was, "I consider Father Capdanno [sic] fit for military service in any area." [177]

The next day, Father Capodanno wrote to the Chief of Chaplains for the United States military, asking for information and stating, "I would like to join the Navy with the intention of serving as a chaplain to the Marine Corps. Is this possible?"[178]

Finally, on July 14th, Father Capodanno communicated his thoughts by cable to his Maryknoll superior, Bishop Comber: "As fulfillment of personal desire and help fill dire need respectfully request permission to join Navy chaplains. Hopefully awaiting

---

[176] AMIL, Box: Correspondence Binder. Kowloon, Hong Kong, August 18, 1965, Father Vincent R. Capodanno, MM, to Lieutenant Commander Carl A. Auel.

[177] AMIL, Box: Chaplaincy & Vietnam Binder. Hong Kong, July 13, 1965, Medical examination results.

[178] AMIL, Box: Correspondence Binder. Kowloon, Hong Kong, July 14, 1965, Father Vincent R. Capodanno, MM, to "Chief of Chaplains, the Pentagon."

permission and your good wishes, Fr. Vincent Capodanno." [179]

The Father General wrote to Father Capodanno on July 17th:

> I received your cablegram about entering the Navy. I am not particularly adverse to you entering the Navy, but I do think you should take your time about such a decision. You first wanted to go back to Taiwan and secondly to be transferred to another Region, and now you want to go to the Navy.

> I can assure you that we want to do everything to help you in making your decision, and so I am asking you to write me a letter telling me about how you feel. I have never had anything from you but very brief letters. It is not a decision which should be made very hurriedly. You also can talk it over with Father McLoughlin or some one of the others there.

> I know that there have been things to irritate you there in the Region, but they should not push you into a decision which may not be a happy one.[180]

Father Capodanno continued his communications with various offices of the United States military, including the office of the Chief of Chaplains in Washington, D.C., trying to elicit specific answers to his earlier questions before he responded to the Father General's letter. In one telegram to the Navy, he requested: "[Maryknoll] Redistribution of personnel urgently requires statement of my future plans respectfully request

---

[179] MFBA, Box: Capodanno Personnel File. Folder: Capodanno, Rev. Vincent R/Documents. Hong Kong, N.d. [July 14, as indicated in the cable], Father Vincent R. Capodanno, MM, to Bishop John W. Comber, MM.

[180] MFBA, Box: Capodanno Personnel File. Folder: Capodanno, Rev. Vincent R/Documents. Maryknoll, July 17, 1965, Bishop John W. Comber, MM, to Father Vincent R. Capodanno, MM.

comment on Medical Report sent you earlier."[181]

Responses from the military and from the Chief of Chaplains came quickly. On July 30th he received a letter from the Navy and on August 2nd a cable from the Chief of Chaplains, both informing him that he must apply for military service at any Navy recruiting station "geographically located in the United States." Likewise, before any official acceptance of his application, the Navy required official ecclesiastical endorsement from his Maryknoll superiors.[182]

As Maryknoll waited for an answer from Father Capodanno to the Father General's letters, Bishop Donaghy wrote Bishop Comber once again:

> As I wrote in the July Diary, during my visit to Hongkong [sic] I had a short talk, it could hardly be termed a conversation. . . two are required for such, with Father Capodanno and, as far AS I WAS CONCERNED, IT WAS COMPLETELY POINTLESS. He told me that he had cabled you but was unwilling to divulge the nature of the cable. All that I gathered from the meeting was that he was adamant in his determination to have a change. He keeps very much to himself and Father McLoughlin told me that following his arrival in Hongkong [sic] he has been out to Stanley [Maryknoll house] only once, and that was to attend the Mass and luncheon for the silver jubilarians.
>
> I still feel, and the consultors share the view, that it would be of highly dubious value to him, and of serious detriment to the work as a whole, to have him return to

---

[181] AMIL, Box: Capodanno Correspondence, 14. Cable, Hong Kong, July 30, 1965, Father Vincent R. Capodanno, MM, to Lieutenant J. Lloyd Dreith.

[182] AMIL, Box: Correspondence Binder. N.p. July 30, 1965, Lieutenant Commander Carl A. Auel to Father Vincent R. Capodanno, MM. AMIL, Box: Capodanno Correspondence 14. Cable: N.p., August 2, 1965, Rear Admiral James W. Kelly to Father Vincent R. Capodanno, MM.

Formosa. . . either to Miaoli or Taichung. And I can honestly state that this opinion is not prompted by meaness [sic], pig-headedness or narrow mindedness.

Re: his joining the Armed Services; personally, I see no objections to yielding to his request and I do not say this merely to advance a quick and easy solution to the case. Certainly, if his present mood or frame of mind perdures he well might prove to be a problem in any mission to which he might be assigned.[183]

The Father General responded:

I wrote to Father Capodanno a few days before I wrote to you and asked him to consider his decision well. Since then I have not heard from him. He seems to prefer cables or twenty word letters where he does not give much news about himself. [184]

Once he had successfully completed his physical examination and gathered information about enlisting in the United States Navy, Father Capodanno wrote Bishop Comber on August 9th, answering the Father General's letters of June 8, July 8 and July 17. He wrote as a man beleaguered and under pressure, yet seeking a mutually satisfactory solution with his superior:

My letters have been brief because I have found that repetition of details in letters can lead to misunderstanding and confusion rather than clarity. I have copies of all my own letters and the responses

---

[183] MFBA, Taiwan Regional Records Correspondence 1960-1968 Box 2. Folder: Taiwan Records 2/7 Regional Superior's Correspondence 1965. Miaoli, August 3, 1965, Bishop Frederick A. Donaghy, MM, to Bishop John W. Comber, MM. [Emphasis in capital letters in original].

[184] MFBA, Taiwan Regional Records Correspondence 1960-1968 Box 2. Folder: Taiwan Records 2/7 Regional Superior's Correspondence 1965. Maryknoll, August 10, 1965, Bishop John W. Comber, MM, to Bishop Frederick A. Donaghy, MM.

thereto as well as copies of conversations written down by me within a few hours after they had taken place. I have summarized in the following paragraph their contents and also the development of my cabled request.

Preceding and within my correspondence with you, there is a logical progression, each step and conclusion of which I carefully considered before initiating, on April 1, my correspondence with the Regional Superior, which I knew would culminate in my correspondence with you, which, itself, would possibly include the cable I eventually did send. After having been refused four times to be transferred from Hong Kong to Taichung, I considered it improper to make the same request of you and unlikely that you would grant it even if I did make it and therefore wrote requesting to be transferred to a different Region. After receiving your replys [sic] of June 8 and July 8, I then requested to join the Chaplain Corps. I felt and do feel that this request, which would keep me in the [Maryknoll] Society where I wish to remain and yet which would effect a necessary change, provides the most personally desirable work and arrangement.

If you grant me permission to join the Navy, as I hope you will, enlistment requires written and official ecclesiastical permission and endorsement to be presented at the time of enlistment.[185]

Father Capodanno continued, stating that he would be required to return to the United States to enlist, and then attend the United States Navy Chaplain's Training School in Newport, Rhode Island: "May I ask you to assign me to Hawaii for enlistment purposes and permit me to spend the waiting period

[185] AMIL, Box: Correspondence Binder. Kowloon, Hong Kong, August 9, 1965, Father Vincent R. Capodanno, MM, to Bishop John W. Comber, MM [copy]. Original in MFBA, Box: Capodanno Personnel Files. Folder: Capodanno, Rev. Vincent R/Documents.

helping out at one of our missions there."

On August 13th, the Father General of Maryknoll wrote granting Father Capodanno permission to apply for a chaplaincy in the United States Navy. "I would prefer that you apply for the Army as there is a greater need there, but you can make this decision yourself." He was assigned to the Maryknoll mission in Hawaii, where he could wait out the six month residency requirement before applying to the military. [186] On the same day, Bishop Comber wrote to the pastor of the Maryknoll parish in Hawaii, assigning Father Capodanno temporarily to his parish, asking the pastor to assist the younger Maryknoll missionary.[187] The Maryknoll General Superior also wrote to Monsignor Joseph F. Marbach of the Military Ordinariate in the Archdiocese of New York, stating that "I am recommending Father Capodanno as a priest of good moral character and one who should be able to give good service in the Armed Forces."[188]

Expressing the general observation about Father Capodanno's situation, held by many of the Maryknoll missioners who worked in Taiwan, Father Elmer P. Wurth, MM, observed, "I think he [Father Capodanno] showed his holiness and strength of character under unfair treatment."[189]

On August 18th, Bishop Comber's letter of permission arrived, and Father Capodanno acknowledged it the same day. Father Capodanno thanked the Father General for his kindness,

---

[186] MFBA, Box: Capodanno Personnel Files. Folder: Capodanno, Rev. Vincent R/Documents. N.p. August 13, 1965, Bishop John W. Comber, MM, to Father Vincent Capodanno, MM.

[187] MFBA, Box: Capodanno Personnel Files. Folder: Capodanno, Rev. Vincent R/Documents. N.p. August 13, 1965, Bishop John W. Comber, MM, to Very Reverend John J. Stankard, MM.

[188] MFBA, Box: Capodanno Personnel Files. Folder: Capodanno, Rev. Vincent R/Documents. N.p. August 13, 1965, Bishop John W. Comber, MM, to Monsignor Joseph F. Marbach.

[189] AMIL, Box: Capodanno, Maryknoll. Kalida, Ohio, April 24, 2014, Father P. Elmer Wurth, MM, to Monsignor Stephen M. DiGiovanni.

and announced that he would leave Hong Kong the next day. "There was no advantage to delay and I was fortunately able to make all the necessary arrangements within several hours after your letter arrived." He told his superior that he presumed on his permission that he might stop over in Japan "to visit with close [Maryknoll] classmates there," and would arrive in Hawaii on the morning of Sunday, August 22nd. He concluded by thanking the Father General, informing him:

> I shall enlist in the Navy with the stated request and intention of serving as chaplain in the Marine Corps who use Navy men since they have no chaplains of their own. I hope to be able to volunteer for immediate duty in Viet Nam, which, according to the Marine Liaison Officer at the American Consulate here, may very likely be granted.[190]

Father Capodanno's decision and request to serve as a chaplain in the United States Armed Forces was understandable. The American military had a great need for Catholic chaplains, especially as the Vietnam War intensified. This need offered Father Capodanno a means to enter an important work while remaining a Maryknoll missioner. As Monsignor James Markham wrote to Bishop Comber after having received his written permission for Father Capodanno to apply for a military chaplaincy, "The shortage of chaplains is indeed a serious problem and we trust that many more priests will volunteer for this important apostolate."[191] Maryknoll had been providing chaplains to the United States military services for years, and some of the missioners ministered to American military personnel and their families at various military bases near

---

[190] MFBA, Box: Capodanno Personnel Files. Folder: Capodanno, Rev. Vincent R/Documents. Kowloon, Hong Kong, August 18, 1965, Father Vincent R. Capodanno, MM, to Bishop John W. Comber, MM.

[191] MFBA, Box: Capodanno Personnel Files. N.p. September 13, 1965, Monsignor James J. Markham to Bishop John W. Comber, MM.

Maryknoll missions around the world.[192] In 1962, the Father General mentioned this in a letter to Bishop Donaghy: "I suppose you realize that Cardinal Spellman is continually needling us for more Maryknollers for the Armed Services." [193] In some way, Father Capodanno's request was also helpful to Maryknoll in its relationship with the Cardinal Archbishop of New York, who was also the Vicar for the Military Ordinariate in the United States, and in whose archdiocese the Maryknoll motherhouse was located in Ossining, New York.

Likewise, the need for Catholic chaplains to minister to the United States Catholic military personnel was immense, precisely at this time. Between late 1964 and the middle of 1965 the United States became more intensely dedicated to the Vietnam War, raising the number of American troops in Vietnam from fifty thousand to ninety thousand during this time. The number would soon rise higher.[194] In his 1965 annual report to the American hierarchy, Cardinal Spellman reiterated the need for Catholic chaplains:

> I have been requested by the military authorities to advise you of the serious situation that exists concerning the spiritual life of our men and women in the Armed Forces. . . .Often I have tried to present to you the thought that it is not a question of charity but a question of justice—we are obliged in justice to provide spiritual care for those who are engaged in the defense of our

---

[192] MFBA, Taiwan Regional Records Correspondence 1960-1968 Box 2. Folder: Taiwan Regional Superior's Correspondence 1962. Maryknoll, February 20, 1962, Very Reverend John F. Donovan, MM, to Bishop Frederick A. Donaghy, MM.

[193] MFBA, Taiwan Regional Records Correspondence 1960-1968 Box 2. Folder: Taiwan Records Regional Superior's Correspondence 1962. Maryknoll, N.d ["Thanks for yours of March 21, 1962"], Bishop John W. Comber, MM, to Bishop Frederick A. Donaghy, MM.

[194] Schulzinger, Robert D., *A Time for War. The United States and Vietnam, 1941-1975* (New York, 1997), p. 154.

country.[195]

Father Capodanno responded to that urgent need. He was spurred on by the unhappy situation created by Bishop Donaghy. The catalyst of the crisis was the Irish-American bishop's insistence that the young Italo-American missionary priest be removed from mission parish work on Taiwan in which he was needed, to teach English in a high school in Hong Kong in which he was not needed.

Father James P. Nieckarz, MM, expressed the view of many Maryknoll missioners at the time:

> I am a Maryknoll Missioner and I love the Society very much. . . But as in most human institutions we, as members, have our faults, prejudices + misunder-standings and some members have been treated poorly at times. Some obeyed, in spite of opposition + many simply left the Society. In my view, Father Vincent was treated poorly, even unjustly. Though, he tried to get a hearing + a transfer to resolve the situation, he was unsuccessful. But he did not condemn or talk badly about other members. And he did not leave Maryknoll. He simply asked to be allowed to become a military chaplain.[196]

A chaplaincy in the United States military provided Father Capodanno with the solution. He was insistent to remain a Maryknoll missionary. By means of a chaplaincy, he could serve the urgent need for Catholic chaplains serving American troops on the battlefields of Vietnam. But, he could do something more. With memories of an earlier generation of Maryknoll missionaries witnessing to Christ before the onslaught of militant atheistic Communism in Asia just ten years earlier, this was an opportunity for him to do the same. The American

---

[195] CUA, NCWC, Annual Reports, Box 68, Folder 12: NCWC Annual Reports, 1965: "Military Ordinariate United States of America, Annual Report, 1965," p. 3.

[196] AMIL, Box: Capodanno, Maryknoll. Staten Island, July 12, 2006, Father James P. Nieckarz, MM, to Mary Preece, p. 5r.

military efforts in Vietnam were seen by many, and touted by the United States government, as part of America's larger Cold War efforts to stem the progress of Communism. American leaders held "that all international events were connected to the Cold War." [197]

To a certain degree, Father Capodanno agreed, as seen in his Vietnam homilies, quoted later in this narrative. However, his service in the United States military was not motivated by politics. While helping to stop the spread of atheistic Communism, he could also be with men who needed God so very desperately on the battlefield. He saw an opportunity to imitate Christ, by laying down his life for others, and he took it.

Once he received written permission from the Father General, Father Capodanno wrote to Lieutenant Commander Carl A. Auel at the Department of the Navy's Bureau of Naval Personnel in Washington, D.C., informing him of his decision, and wrote, "I do not know if this will have any efficacy, but on the presumption that it might, may I say that I hope I shall be granted immediate duty in Viet Nam upon completion of Training School in Rhode Island."[198]

Immediately after arriving in Honolulu, Father Capodanno consulted with the local Marine Recruiting Office, "and have since then been filling out the proper forms and reporting for interviews." In his enthusiasm, he tried to meet all requirements as soon as possible. Reporting to Bishop Comber, he narrated everything he had been doing since his arrival, trying his best to fulfill all the requirements given him by the personnel at the recruiting office. Father Capodanno also informed the Father General that he named him and another priest as character references, and that "you will probably be

---

[197] Schulzinger, *A Time for War,* p. 329.

[198] AMIL, Box: Correspondence Binder. Kowloon, Hong Kong, August 18, 1965, Father Vincent R. Capodanno, MM, to Lieutenant Commander Carl A. Auel.

soon contacted by the FBI." [199] In the "Statement of Personal History" portion of his application to the Navy, Father Capodanno listed Bishop William Kupfer, MM, under the category of "Friends" who could recommend him. He also listed Father J. Donald McGinnis, MM, in the Maryknoll mission in Tahu, Miaoli, and Father Howard D. Trube, MM, in Hong Kong. He did not list Bishop Frederick Donaghy, MM, who had been Father Capodanno's Regional Superior during his years in Taiwan and Hong Kong. [200]

Father General wrote on September 4th to both the Military Ordinariate granting his permission, and to Father Capodanno, instructing him to apply for a chaplaincy through the offices of the Military Ordinariate, and suggested to the enthusiastic missioner, "I think this is better than dealing with the ordinary recruiting office." [201]

Later in August, 1965, Father Capodanno wrote a lengthy letter to his family, mailed through the Naval recruiting office in Honolulu, which traveled via Camp Pendleton, California. The first page of the letter responded to a number of family letters that he had been unable to answer during the previous hectic weeks. The final two pages filled in the details of the summer's events, his decision to apply for a chaplaincy in the military, and his transfer to Hawaii. [202]

While in Hawaii, Father Capodanno worked and lived in

[199] MFBA, Box: Capodanno Personnel Files. Folder: Capodanno, Rev. Vincent R/Documents. Honolulu, Hawaii, August 30, 1965, Father Vincent R. Capodanno, MM, to Bishop John W. Comber, MM.

[200] CAP/Staten, N.p. August 31, 1965, Father Vincent R. Capodanno: "Statement of Personal History," p. 2.

[201] MFBA, Box: Capodanno Personnel Files. Folder: Capodanno. Maryknoll, September 4, 1965, Bishop John W. Comber to Monsignor Joseph F. Marbach; MFBA, as above, N.p. September 4, 1965, Bishop John W. Comber, MM, to Father Vincent R. Capodanno, MM.

[202] CAP/Staten, Fld MedSerCol—B66, Marine Corps Base, Camp Pendleton, CA, August 29, 1965, Father Vincent R. Capodanno, MM, to "Dear Dot and Tony and Everyone."

the Maryknoll parish at Kamueal, awaiting his acceptance by the military. One day, after offering Mass, Father Capodanno met an American couple. Years later, they wrote about the priest and his sermon to one of Father Vincent's brothers, James Capodanno:

> His Mass in itself was very special. His sermon dealt with the conditions in Taiwan and his own plan to go to Vietnam. I recall vividly thinking, 'why?' For he had already done so much in the Orient and he had the dedication and power to reach people here at home. So many choose to remain ignorant of conditions elsewhere. They have to be reached in order to have them act. For our world problems will be solved by straight thinkers with dedication and compassion, not on the battle ground. But it was obvious that your brother wanted desperately to be where he could really help those who couldn't help themselves.[203]

A few months after Father Capodanno's death in Vietnam, a fellow Maryknoll missioner wrote Father Vincent's sister, Pauline, with the reason given him by Father Capodanno for his choice to become a military chaplain in Vietnam: "I do recall that he felt there was a pressing need in Vietnam at the moment, and he felt called to serve that need."[204]

By September 14th, the Military Ordinariate informed Father Capodanno that he had been granted permission to apply for a chaplaincy in the Naval Reserve.[205] By September 23rd, Monsignor Markham informed both the Chief of Chaplains and Father Capodanno that ecclesiastical endorsement had been

---

[203] CAP/Staten, San Rafael, California, January 21, 1969, Mrs. Jean Desmond Mactavish to James Capodanno.

[204] MFBA, Box: Capodanno Personnel Files. Folder: Capodanno, Rev. Vincent R/Documents, N.p., November 14, 1967, Father John J. McCormack, MM, to Mrs. Pauline Costa.

[205] CAP/Staten, N.p., September 14, 1965, Monsignor James J. Markham to Father Vincent R. Capodanno, MM.

granted him by the Military Ordinariate.[206]

On November 22nd, the Chief of Chaplains wrote Father Capodanno informing him that his application had been accepted:

> Favorable consideration of your application is an indication of our estimate of your abilities and of our trust in your motivation and desire to serve the men and women of the U. S. Navy and Marine Corps. I am confident that you will fulfill our high expectations.
>
> Your request for active duty has also been favorably considered. With your concurrence we expect that you will be ordered to the Chaplain School class convening at the Naval Schools Command, Newport, Rhode Island, on 3 January 1966.
>
> I look forward to welcoming you to our Corps with the prayer that God will richly bless you as you assume this new responsibility.[207]

On November 29th, Father Capodanno received his first assignment as a chaplain from the Military Ordinariate. He was granted personal parochial jurisdiction and faculties necessary for his new priestly ministry while at the Naval School in Newport, Rhode Island, as outlined in the 1961 edition of the *Vademecum For Priests Serving in the Military Vicariate of The United States of America.* [208]

Father Capodanno responded to the Chief of Chaplain's letter on December 9th, writing:

---

[206] CAP/Staten, New York, September 23, 1965, Monsignor James J. Markham to Rear Admiral James W. Kelly. CAP/Staten, N.p., September 23, 1965, Monsignor James J. Markham to Father Vincent R. Capodanno, MM.

[207] Cap/Staten. November 22, 1965, Rear Admiral James W. Kelly to Father Vincent R. Capodanno, MM.

[208] CAP/Staten, New York, November 29, 1965, Chaplain Delegate to Father Vincent R. Capodanno, MM.

My present duties will keep me here in Waimea on the Big Island until December 26 on which day I'll leave Honolulu. According to present plans, my pre-induction physical will take place on Monday, December 27 followed by induction on December 29. Transportation arrangements are now being made and I will leave ample time to report on January 3, 1966 at Newport, Rhode Island.[209]

Father Capodanno was 36 years old.

---

[209] AMIL, Box: Correspondence Binder. Waimea Catholic Church, Kanuela, Hawaii, December 9, 1965, Father Vincent R. Capodanno, MM, to Rear Admiral James W. Kelly.

Chapter V

Training and Vietnam, 1966

Father Vincent Capodanno arrived at the Newport Naval Base in Newport, Rhode Island, on January 3, 1966. His new identity as a Catholic chaplain with the rank of Lieutenant was made clear by his Smythson's *Featherweight Diary*, on which he had imprinted "Lt. Vincent Capodanno" instead of "Rev. Vincent Capodanno," as on the covers of his earlier diaries.[210] He used these diaries, not to record upcoming appointments, but to record random ideas and notes for homilies, names, addresses and phone numbers, lists of needed items, such as "plastic water and wine" bottles for Mass [April 6, 1965], or "insect repellant" [January 1, 1966]. Most important, once in Vietnam, he used the diaries to record names, ranks, serial numbers of soldiers, their wounds, battles in which they fought, and the home contact information of parents and families.

His eight-week course of studies in Newport taught him and his classmates the basic practices and concepts of Navy life, as well as the requirements and expectations for working with chaplains and soldiers of all religions in the American military services.

After completing the course of study on February 24, 1966, the Thursday after Ash Wednesday, Father Capodanno was granted leave to visit his family. He stayed with his sister Pauline and her family in Kearny, New Jersey, offering daily Mass at the local parish of Mary Queen of Peace in Arlington. This was the parish church from which he would be buried the next year. On February 27th, he baptized his niece Pauline Mary, "The only baby he baptized in the family."[211]

---

[210] AMIL: Box: Correspondence Binder. *Featherweight Diary*, 1965.

[211] AMIL, Box: Correspondence Binder. N.p., February 23, 1967, Father Vincent R. Capodanno, MM, to "Kathleen, Al and Gang." The above quotation is a handwritten note at the bottom of this letter, written by Kathleen Capodanno.

His next assignment was to Camp Pendleton, California. He received the usual "personal parochial jurisdiction" from the Military Ordinariate on March 10th. His unit jurisdiction was the 3rd Marine Division; his territorial jurisdiction was Camp Pendleton, Camp Del Mar & Camp Stuart Mesa, California. [212] He arrived at Camp Pendleton on *Laetare* Sunday, March 16, 1966, to begin a three week course at the Field Medical Service School. There he trained in battlefield first aid and tactics and survival skills, along with a regimen of physical training and exercise.

He wrote his brother James and his family, briefly describing his first days at Camp Pendleton, where his brother had trained as a Marine during World War II. Nearly half the group of chaplains, including himself, had no military experience, ". . . and in the beginning, the drill classes looked something like the Marx Brothers running around. The DI [Drill Instructor] was a long, lean well-seasoned Marine but even he nearly doubled up with laughter one morning."[213]

Both Passion and Palm Sundays were spent at Camp Pendleton. Father Capodanno offered Mass for the local troops, and completed his training on April 6th, Wednesday of Holy Week. In preparation for his departure for Okinawa and Vietnam, the Military Ordinariate granted him faculties and "personal parochial jurisdiction" over the 3rd Marine Division, with territorial jurisdiction over "All subjects of the Military Vicar assigned to or residing in Okinawa—also in Vietnam if this is the assignment."[214]

His first Easter in the military was celebrated in Washington, D.C., where Father Capodanno awaited transport to Vietnam. The next day, Easter Monday, he purchased a travel

---

[212] AMIL, Box: Capodanno Official Records 1. New York, March 10, 1966, Father Francis E. Moriarity, CSSR to Father Vincent R. Capodanno, MM.

[213] CAP/Staten, N.p., April 19, 1966, Father Vincent R. Capodanno, MM, to "Lyd and Jim, Vin + Jimmy."

[214] CAP/Staten, New York, March 31, 1966, Father Francis E. Moriarty, CSSR to Father Vincent R. Capodanno, MM.

insurance policy at the local offices of Mutual of Omaha, and sent it to his sister Pauline, asking her to "please save it since it covers my travels for about <u>13 months</u>." He continued, "All is well—I'm off for a cup of coffee + then on to a plane. We fly from here to Tokyo (<u>not</u> Honolulu) + then on to Okinawa."[215] He wrote that he planned to contact two Maryknoll priest friends, Fathers Richard Murto, MM, and James Byrne, MM, once he landed in Japan.

Father Capodanno flew from Travis Air Force Base to Okinawa, and then on to Vietnam,

> . . . on a C-124, one of those huge double-decker cargo planes. In accordance with the usual military protocol, the officers (8) boarded first and ended up sitting between the wings and therefore between the four engines that roared for the next seven hours. The canvas bucket seats lined the sides of the plane leaving the center wide open . . . but not for long; we left at about 05:00 after being picked up at 00:30 and within minutes after takeoff the center aisle was packed with sprawling Marines— enlisted, NCO's [non-commissioned officers] and officers alike. Sounds rough but was actually not too bad and everyone slept well and long. [216]

His temporary assignment was to Chu Lai, Vietnam, at the Danang Enclave, living in a "transients' tent until I receive a specific assignment." [217] He shared the tent with three civilians and one Marine Major, all engineers. The men had an electric fan, and Father Capodanno purchased one in Okinawa, "so we are even cool," he reported to his family. Father Vincent was assigned as the chaplain to the 1st Battalion, 7th Marines

---

[215] AMIL, Box: Correspondence Binder. Washington, D.C., April 11, 1966, Father Vincent R. Capodanno, MM, to Pauline + George.

[216] CAP/Staten, N.p. April 19, 1966, Father Vincent R. Capodanno, MM, to "Lyd and Jim, Vin + Jimmy."

[217] CAP/Staten, Ibid.

[referred to by the Marines as 1/7]. There were three Marine battalions [1/7, 2/7 and the 3/7] situated around the Chu Lai airfield, and Father Capodanno, being the only Catholic chaplain for the 7th Marines, was busy attending to the spiritual needs of the Marines in all three battalions. He reported to the Chaplain Delegate to Cardinal Spellman, "The work is most rewarding and even though I am busy as the only Catholic chaplain in the 7th Reg., I enjoy every minute of it."[218] He visited the city of Danang on April 18th, going with two other chaplains to make a donation to the Sacred Heart Orphanage:

> We went in (the orphanage is in the heart of the town next to the cathedral), visited with the kids and nuns for a few moments, left and returned with no difficulty. . . even got a big wave from one of the VN (Vietnamese) generals who was going into town in his staff-car. [219]

Father Capodanno's first experience of battle came the next month, May 10-15, 1966: Operation Montgomery/Lien Kat 40 was a security operation in the Quang Ngai Province, involving 1/5, 1/7, 2/7 of the United States Marines, along with the 2nd and 5th Marine Battalions of the Republic of Vietnam (VNMC). Father Capodanno was assigned to the Battalion Aid Station. Chaplain Roy Baxter recalled the priest's heroism during the military operation:

> During the first night [of battle], the VC [Viet Cong] had come out of a well-concealed network of cunningly devised tunnels in strategic proximity to the Battalion CP (Command Post) bivouac and launched a grenade assault. Without regard for his own safety, Vince [Capodanno] exposed himself [to enemy fire] while he held a flashlight for the corpsmen treating the casualties. . . From the very

[218] AMIL, Box: Correspondence Binder. San Francisco, May 31, 1966, Father Vincent R. Capodanno, MM, to Father Francis E. Moriarity, CSSR.
[219] CAP/Staten, N.p., April 19, 1966, Father Vincent R. Capodanno, MM, to "Lyd and Jim, Vin + Jimmy" Capodanno.

outset, I was impressed that Vince possessed the desirable quality of poise—which was characteristically manifest throughout my tour with him. [220]

His next experience of battle came at the end of the month: May 25-28, during Operation Mobile, which was a search and destroy mission in the Quang Ngai Province, involving the 1/7 of the United States Marines, along with the 5th Marine Battalion of the Republic of Vietnam (VNMC).

He wrote his brother Albert and his family, but made no mention of the military operations, telling them, "Everything is going along very well here." He then told them something of his work:

> I had an opportunity this morning to visit and say Mass at one of our sub-units stationed already on the other side of the river. I can't always get out there, but the Colonel was going and invited me along. I may be able to get back there next week, too. When I returned, had lunch and then off to the sub-unit at which I had arranged to say Mass this afternoon, then back, shower, supper and evening Mass here followed by an instruction class which ended just a few minutes ago at 9 PM. This is not my average day but it does explain why this is going to be a brief letter![221]

While he was typing this letter, a Marine came to his tent, who obviously wanted to sit and speak with the chaplain. Father Capodanno continued his letter to his brother, describing an aspect of his work with the Marines that would become essential:

> Well, someone stopped in to see me to discuss something. I stayed at my typewriter as long as I could, but he stayed,

---

[220] Quoted in Mode, *The Grunt Padre*, p. 92.

[221] AMIL, Box: Correspondence Binder. N.p. June 14, 1966, Father Vincent R. Capodanno, MM, to "Kathleen and Al & Kids."

too, so I sat and talked with him. He ended the conversation by asking if I had ever written a book and I almost said something about my unfinished letter, much less a book. He left a few minutes after.

Father Capodanno concluded this letter to his brother with his usual promise, "I remember everyone at Mass. Keep me in your own prayers." Likewise, this letter reveals the generosity that Father Vincent inspired in his family and friends back home. In response to the priest's requests, they frequently sent gifts to Father Capodanno's Marines: cigarettes, cigarette lighters, candy, clothing, rain coats, and various other things that gave some happiness and a modicum of comfort to the Marines about to go into battle in Vietnam.

A former Marine, Ray J. Savage, recalled the early months serving with Father Capodanno:

> Chaplain Capodanno and I joined 1st Battalion, 7th Marine Regiment in May 1966. He was Battalion Chaplain, and myself as the Communication Officer. I remember Vince as a rather quiet, sincere and extremely dedicated person—a little older and more mature than most of the officers in the Battalion. He was to me the epitome of a Marine Chaplain.

> I recall that during staff briefings prior to an operation, Chaplain Capodanno always inquired of the intelligence officer which Company would more likely be most exposed to enemy fire and subject to the highest casualties. That would be the one Chaplain Capodanno placed himself with.

> During any operation of more than two or three days duration, Chaplain Capodanno would manage to hop a ride, by whatever means available, to each Company as well as the Battalion Command Group to talk with the men and officers and to minister in whatever way the situation called for. I think he had a great calming effect

on all those with whom he came in contact. The ministry of presence was no better demonstrated by any chaplain I have ever been associated with than Chaplain Capodanno.[222]

His earlier personal habits instilled in him by his family, the disciplined life developed during his seminary years, and the deepening of faith and charity during his mission years in Taiwan, tested in the crucible of conflict with his Maryknoll superiors, prepared him for his ministry in the muddy battlefields and primitive conditions of Vietnam. The needs of his Marines took precedence over all else in his priestly life, and his native generosity was given free reign of expression in his new priestly ministry.

By July, 1966, he still had not moved across the river. He wrote his brother James and his family:

> The new area is being worked on and the sites for the various buildings have already been assigned. . . the colonel gave the choicest site to the chapel. We are going to have a new chapel of bamboo and thatch built beginning early next week. It will be the same size as the present one, 16 feet wide and 48 long but will be much better since it will be new. [223]

July 26-28 was the next military engagement for Father Capodanno and his Marines: Operation Franklin/Operation Lien Ket 50. Another search and destroy operation in the Quang Ngai Province, involving the 1/7, 2/7 Battalions of the United States Marines, along with the 2nd Division of the Army of the Republic of Vietnam (ARVN). A few days later, Father Capodanno wrote his Marine brother James and his family,

> . . . we have finally moved across the river and things are

---

[222] CAP/Staten, N.p., May Day, 1987, Ray J. Savage to Father R.E. Sheridan, MM.

[223] CAP/Staten, N.p. July 16, 1966, Father Vincent R. Capodanno, MM, to "Lyd, Jim, Vin, Jimmy" Capodanno.

not quite settled yet. I am going out to one of the line companys [sic] for Mass and will stay overnight so I am trying to get this note done.[224]

The new command post was dedicated on August 17th, the birthday of the 7th Marines, during which Father Capodanno preached. He spoke about a common experience of Marines in Vietnam, and, sometimes, of priests: [225]

> It is pointless to say I don't like it here and will do my best elsewhere. Belief in Christ brings with it a deeply rooted sense of the primacy and urgency of now. Not last year or next year, but now. Each of us has been given talents and ability by Almighty God. We should ask ourselves if we are using these to the best of our ability. If we don't use them here, chances are we'll not use them elsewhere either. There will always be an excuse.
>
> And it is now that we must consider and appreciate and review our own talents and gifts we have received from the hand of God himself. Properly understood we can be proud of them, but never haughty about them. They are given to us for our own benefit and that of others.
>
> Putting this into the very, very present tense, we should not look down upon the Vietnamese because they do not have all the gifts and blessings we ourselves have.
>
> What is required of us is the patient <u>and</u> intelligent use of our obvious superiority in so many fields. Not as if we ourselves are solely responsible for these gifts but as instruments of God who has given these gifts to us for our own benefit and for the benefit of others as well.

---

[224] CAP/Staten, N.p. August 4, 1966, Father Vincent R. Capodanno, MM, to "Lyd and Jim" Capodanno.

[225] AMIL, Box: Correspondence Binder. August 17, 1966, Father Vincent R. Capodanno, MM. "Sermon for the Regimental Birthday and Blessing of the New Command Post."

We are not here to engender a feeling of jealousy because of what we have or hatred because we use our gifts perhaps in a very obnoxious way.

We can be compared to adults, and the VN [Vietnamese] to children, but both created by God who is vitally interested in both.

Because of the extremely limited material and spiritual gifts the VN have, we can say they are the least of Christ's brethren...

The Regimental birthday and the dedication of the new CP [Command Post] represent a fitting occasion for each of us to do a little analyzing to see if we are using here and now the gifts God has given us in the way he intends for us to use them.

Lord God, Heavenly Father, we ask your blessing on our new CP and the entire BN [Battalion] that we may serve you with faith, our country with loyalty and our BN with courage.

Through your grace and blessing may each of us contribute a spirit of kindness and mature understanding for each other and for the Vietnamese people among whom we are now living.

And Lord God, with pride in their sacrifice and sadness at their absence, we ask your mercy for those of 1/7 who have died. Through your blessing may we be ever inspired by their sacrifice and mindful of the debt we owe them and their families. Keep them in your love and mercy, O Lord, and keep them in our memories that they may be to us a standard for our own efforts. On this day of dedication, God our Father, we beg your blessing on our new CP and all the members of the BN, both living and dead. We ask this through Jesus Christ your Son, Our Lord. Amen.

During the summer of 1966, Eugene S. Jones, the renowned American director-producer, assisted by two college technicians, spent 97 days filming Mike Company of 3/7 Marines. They lived in the camps and foxholes, walked on patrol, and went into the battlefields with the Marines. The result was one of the great American classic documentaries of the Vietnam War, *A Face of War*. There is no narration, music, or written dialogue. It is an unscripted film record of the Marines' lives in Vietnam; "As such, it is a sermon on human waste that draws the viewer into the void as objectively as any war movie ever made."[226] This documentary helped fuel the growing American opposition to the Vietnam War. One scene shows Father Capodanno offering Mass outside his tent for those Marines preparing to go off to another military operation, and possible death. A portion of his homily is captured and preserved in the documentary. Father Capodanno presented to his Marines the realities of God's will, life and death:

> Any little bit of joy or happiness that we have here is but a taste of the eternal happiness we're going to have in heaven. But in order to achieve that eternal life in heaven, we must go through the process that we have come to call death. God has given us life that we should live it fully, live it completely, live it happily. God chooses the minute for each death and uses various circumstances to achieve that."

By this time, Father Capodanno had established his *modus operandi*. His tent was at the headquarters of the 7th Battalion. There, he prayed daily, offered Mass each morning, and gave soldiers instructions in the Catholic faith. He visited the sick and dying, traveled to speak with the Marines in the other nearby Battalions, and, in the evenings, typed his letters to Marine families, to his own family, and made himself available to any Marine who needed counseling. Early on in his tour of duty,

---

[226] *New York Times*, May 11, 1968: Movie review, Howard Thompson, *A Face of War (1967)*.

Father Capodanno began joining his Marines on patrol and on the battlefield, unlike other chaplains. There, often under heavy fire, he risked his life to attend to wounded Marines, calmed their fears, bolstered their faith, prepared them to die, and administered the Last Rites to Catholics. He described his days and work to an American reporter, Kenneth Armstrong, who included his interview with Father Capodanno in his article that ran in September, 1966, as part of a series about the war:

> NAM TRAM PENINSULA, South Viet Nam—Up and down the Marine column, I head the whispered words, 'The padre's coming with us!' And the reaction 'Number 1!'
>
> The padre, the armed forces term for a chaplain, whether Protestant, Catholic or Jewish, was a tanned and fit Maryknoll Father, Navy Lieutenant Vincent Capodanno of Staten Island, N.Y.
>
> Superficially, he could not be distinguished from other officers. He did not wear insignia of rank. That is standard in the field—the Viet Cong concentrates its fire at officers—but everybody in Alpha Company, 1st Battalion 7th Regiment Marines, knew who he was.
>
> AS WE HIKED with the Marines that sweltering day, we had a chance to talk during the occasional rest breaks. Like the Marines, he had a crewcut under his helmet but unlike the young Leathernecks, his hair was stained with gray, a hint of his age, 37.
>
> He wore a flak jacket, normal equipment for the Marines, and I kidded him 'Father, that's not a very good advertisement for your faith—that flak jacket!'
>
> Laughing, he replied: 'I know it, but it's protective coloration so I blend in with the men. In addition, I understand their trials better if I accept the same burdens they do, such as wearing the jacket and carrying a pack.'
>
> A ONETIME MISSIONARY in Taiwan and Hong

Kong, Fr. Capodanno volunteered for service in January, and after five weeks of physical conditioning at Camp Pendleton, Calif., was assigned Catholic chaplain for the 7th Marine Regiment at Chu Lai. His schedule is hectic.

'My tent is at 1st Battalion headquarters, and I conduct Mass there each morning. But during the day, I circulate among all the battalions,' he said.

'Sunday is my busiest day, of course, and I serve at least three masses—at regimental headquarters and at two or more battalions. In a week, I hold a minimum of 15 masses.'

'HOW OFTEN DO you go on operations?' I asked.

'I make all battalion-size operations,' he replied, 'and as many company-size as possible.'

'Why?'

'Well, I want to be available in the event anything serious occurs; to learn firsthand the problems of the men, and to give them moral support, to comfort them with my presence.

'In addition, I feel I must personally witness how they react under fire—and experience it myself—to understand the fear they feel.'

'Have you been ambushed yet?' I asked

'NO,' HE ANSWERED seriously, 'just general fire. And believe me, I was frightened! You have no idea where it's coming from or who it's aimed at. And like everybody else, I dread the possibility of stepping on a booby trap.'

'What is the general attitude toward religion of these young Marines?'

'Very healthy,' he answered, 'by both Catholics and Protestants.'

'Sometimes, that's hard to believe,' I countered, 'in view of the language I often hear!'

Chuckling, he commented: 'I know what you mean. I thought I knew all the bad words, but I've learned a few new ones over here! However, their swearing is frequently a release. They don't realize what they're saying.'

'DO MANY OF THEM come to you with problems?'

'They certainly do. I spend much of my time counseling, discussing their problems with them.'

'What kind of problems?' I inquired.

'The usual ones. Mainly, problems at home with their family, a wife or a girlfriend. Surprisingly, the biggest problem is when a boy doesn't get any mail from home.'

'Do they ever discuss the moral issue of killing?'

'No, I don't think anyone has ever raised it. To them, this is a job—a nasty job—and that's part of it. Prior to a big operation, some will come to me, but primarily to reinforce their faith.'

'WHAT ABOUT our involvement in Viet Nam?' I asked. 'Do they question it?'

'No, they accept it as a necessary evil of the world today,' he replied. 'And their courage! It's unbelievable. Whether it's going into combat, on patrol, or entering a Viet Cong cave not knowing what's below!'

During the long sweep through the wilting heat, Fr. Capodanno never faltered. It was apparent that the Marines were pleased with his presence.

Near the end of the long day, a few approached and shyly said, 'Padre, thanks for coming. It meant a lot to us to have you along.'

115

He answered with a grin, 'In a way, it was very selfish of me, because I really enjoyed being with you.'

And he meant it.[227]

Soon after this article was published, Father Capodanno joined the Marines of 1/7 in Operation Fresno, September 8-16, 1966. It was another search and destroy mission in the Quang Nagai Province, which took place as the North Vietnamese forces worked to disrupt Vietnamese national elections. For his efforts on the battlefield, Father Capodanno was awarded the Vietnamese Cross of Gallantry with Silver Star by the Republic of Vietnam. The October 17, 1966 citation read:

> Lieutenant CAPODANNO is an excellent Chaplain. During the Operation FRESNO, he disregarded all difficulties to go to the front line in order to console, excite the spirit and increase the combat morale of all operational units. He shared a remarkable merit in the triumph. [228]

The reception of military awards was not the heart of Father Capodanno's life. In fact, he never informed his family that he received them; they learned of these citations and awards only after his death. Christ and his Marines were the heart of his life and ministry. Following one of the military operations, Father Capodanno preached a memorial sermon to his 7th Marines:

> We are assembled to pay homage to men we knew and admired.
>
> God loved them or they would not have been born: God called them <u>when they were most prepared to go</u>.
>
> Do not let their names become empty memories.

---

[227] *Cleveland Plain Dealer*, September 4, 1966, Kenneth Armstrong, "Padre is 7th Regiment Marines' Morale Booster on Cong Hunt," p. 3 [Emphasis is original].

[228] CAP/Staten, "Republic of Vietnam: Gallantry Cross Citation, October 17, 1966." Authentication Number 681 APO: 4.277, 17 Oct 1966, Pers-G24-0s 17 May 1967.

Recall to mind all their good points, all the many things we admired in them.

Imitate them. In that way their lives will be perpetuated among us.

Our monument to them will not be of bronze or marble, but <u>the living monument of all the good we say of them</u>.[229]

Later in September, Father Capodanno was engaged in another operation designed to foil the North Vietnamese efforts to disrupt the national elections by destroying the rice harvest. Operation Golden Fleece, September 16-27, was carried out by the 1/7, along with the 4th Regiment of the Army of the Republic of Vietnam (ARVN) in the Mo Duc District around the village of Van Ha, about forty miles south of Chu Lai. For his role in both operation Fresno and Golden Fleece, Father Capodanno was awarded the Vietnamese Cross of Gallantry with Bronze Star by the Republic of Vietnam "for meritorious services rendered during Operation FRESNO and GOLDEN FLEECE."[230]

Two days after Operation Golden Fleece, another article about Father Capodanno was filed. This time by a reporter from The Marine Corps Press, which published its article, *Chaplain, Ex-Taiwan Missionary Feels His Job is With Viet Troops*. The article reflected Operation Golden Fleece, and Father Capodanno's reasons for joining the Navy and serving the Marines:

CHU LAI, Vietnam, Sept. 18—He moved quietly from one wounded Marine to another speaking softly to each man.

Wearing no weapon, his hands were stained with

---

[229] AMIL, Box: Funeral Binder, September 19, 1967, Quoted in the Funeral Mass Eulogy by Chaplain Eli Takesian [Emphasis original].

[230] CAP/Staten, Headquarters, 7th Marines, San Francisco, May 4, 1967, Major E.F. Fitzgerald by direction of the Commanding Officer, 7th Marines to VR Capodanno. CAP/Staten, N.p. May 17, 1967, Chief of Naval Personnel to Lt. Robert Vincent [sic] Capodanno, CHC, USNR: "Vietnamese Gallantry Cross with Bronze Star: information concerning." Awarded, November 1, 1966.

blood where he had rested a comforting palm on a critically wounded Marine's head.

Over one Marine he said the last rites and then sat back exhausted watching the helicopters medically evacuate the last of the wounded.

A splotch of blood was caked on his forehead where he had wiped sweat from his brow during the aftermath of a Viet Cong booby trap explosion.

Chaplain (Lt.) Vincent R. Capodanno, 37, of New York City [sic], wears no physical weapon of war.

HIS ARMAMENT is faith—a basic, necessary and treasured attribute to the men around him. He is one of 20 Navy Chaplains serving in the 1st Marine Division and one of 63 in the III Marine Amphibious Force.

When the 1st Bn. [Battalion], Seventh Marine Regiment goes to the field, Chaplain Capodanno goes with them.

He moves among the men, changing companies from day to day so he can be with each unit for some time.

He is new to the service life, but not to the primitive situation that Vietnam lends.

Before joining the Navy Chaplain's Corps in December 1965, Lieutenant Capodanno served 6 ½ years as a missionary in Taiwan, Nationalist China.

He worked with the natives, high in Taiwan's mountainous regions.

'THIS KIND of life isn't new to me,' he said during a recent operation. 'In Taiwan our missionary program was somewhat like the civil affairs program in Vietnam. We moved from village to village, living quite basic most of the time.'

Chaplain Capodanno speaks one Chinese dialect. He belongs to the Catholic Foreign Missionary Society and is a Maryknoll Father dedicated to spreading the faith in the Far East.

'My job here in the field with the men is kind of a morale booster. I'm around if they want to talk and I try to speak with as many of them as possible,' he said.

'I joined the Chaplain Corps when the Vietnam War broke out because I think I'm needed here as are many more chaplains. I'm glad to help in the way I can.'

As he moves among the men of the 1st Battalion, the talk is not always of religion. There is simple talk of men's hopes and aspirations, of men's strength's and weaknesses—all weighed and carefully surmised by the combat assigned chaplain.

There always seems to be a place reserved beside a wounded Marine—a place reserved for Chaplain Capodanno who always seems to appear at the stricken Marine's side to speak or pray at the moment it is most needed. [231]

In his monthly report to the Military Ordinariate, Father Capodanno commented about his men and his work:

All is well here. Even the weather. . . no one quite knows what became of the Monsoons but they are apparently lost somewhere. We have had almost two weeks of good weather interrupted only now and then by half-hearted rains. Militarily, things are going along much as you read about them in the papers. The morale is good and the morals in many, many instances nothing short of exemplary and inspiring. Really.

A Chaplain's work has only one disappointing

---

[231] *The American Weekend*, October 19, 1966, p. 5 [Emphasis is original].

aspect: the days are too short and the time moves too quickly for the men to do all there is to be done. [232]

Father Capodanno was invited to deliver a paper about American military personnel in their relations with the Vietnamese people. His years of experience working in Taiwan provided him with insights that proved unique among Americans, and were invaluable in attempting to create a distinction in the minds of the Marines between the Vietcong whom they fought, and the Vietnamese people caught in the fighting. His paper was entitled, *Some Reflections on Adaptation to the Orient,* and was delivered in the command post in Chu Lai. He wrote,

> It is most necessary for us to remember the influences that have gone into our own formation and equally necessary for us to make an intelligent effort to understand the people in whose homeland we are living.[233]

He wrote that the culture shock experienced by American servicemen coming to Asia for the first time was understandable and could be remedied "by adaptation and acclimatization." He offered "three general areas wherein adjustment to the Orient can be effected more smoothly and gracefully. They are: respect for persons; respect for authority; respect for things." In describing each, Father Capodanno revealed his experience having worked for years with people in small villages in Taiwan. Respect for persons meant that American Marines should first approach and treat with dignity the elders of any village, and not to approach the children first, offering gifts. Once a working relationship based upon respect and authority was established, the Marines' work would prove easier. This reflected the second

---

[232] AMIL, Box: Correspondence Binder. San Francisco, November 4, 1966, Father Vincent R. Capodanno, MM, to Father Joseph F. Marbach.

[233] AMIL, Box: Correspondence Binder. Father Vincent R. Capodanno, MM, "Some Reflections on Adaptation to the Orient," p. 3-4. See Appendix II.

principle, respect for authority, whereby a Marine officer would treat directly with the village elder to enlist his cooperation before giving orders to his Marines. Respect for things was based on the earlier principles:

> When the materially poor see carelessness in the use and distribution of things and money the natural conclusion is that the materially richer are behaving foolishly. A further conclusion is that the foolish merit neither respect nor consistent cooperation.

The Force Chaplain, J. H. Craven, requested a copy, which Father Capodanno sent in mid-November, commenting:

> The thoughts contained in this paper are my own and although they have been verbally articulated I have not before written them down. Because of their familiarity they do not have the impact on me that perhaps they have or will have on others. I am not as immediately receptive to their inaccuracies as others who are hearing them for the first time in this format might be. I hold them only as opinions and am open to their further development and growth and change.[234]

Some of the thoughts expressed in his paper were included in a sermon he delivered to the Marines in Vietnam at the same time anti-war protests were becoming more frequent and strident in the United States. His sermon notes reveal his own reflections about the war, and his role as a chaplain to men in war, while treating of the difficult question of the Marines' moral responsibility during battle. The sermon is interesting on many levels, including his use of abbreviations, symbols and colors to remind him to use special emphasis while delivering the sermon:

> Mature consideration for others whether we like

---

[234] AMIL, Box: Correspondence. 1st Bn. 7th Marines, San Francisco, November 15, 1966, Father Vincent R. Capodanno, MM, to Chaplain J. H. Craven.

them or not, based on extraordinary consideration God [triangle] has for us.

[Red]: How can minds be on God's truths in a combat zone? Mst [must] attempt to inc [incorporate] nolege [knowledge] of Xt [Christ] as we inc in all other nolege.

[Green]: Mre [more] exposed to life's complexities—nat<u>al</u> [natural], normal that we achieve greater facility in the art of lving. [living]

[Red]: Easily made decisions—only black + white—take on new depth—recognize lrge [large] grey area where we do mst [most] of our living—most of our groping.

[Green]: Unfortunately, in grey area where we also experience mst of our religious confusion.

[Red]: Lerned [learned] blk + whte [black + white] now realize grey is predominant. We learned principles + now mst apply them. We received the tiny seed that we mst nourish so it will Grow into Great Tree of Faith.

[Green]: Today's Mass Prayer—How do it in a combat zone? Disobedient? Guilty of murder? If only black + white—only confusion. If try to understand—try to apply Prins. [principles] Can resolve confusion.

[Red]: Right to defend property-life ± our way of life. Everyone has these rights. A DEMOCRATIC way of life based on belief in God has an unassailable right to defend itself from atheism + an impractical economic system. It has also the obligation to make its own way of life available to others so they can intelligently accept or refuse it. [It] is what we are doing here in VN. [Vietnam]

[Green]: In course of action people killed. Not because we deliberately want to deprive them of life—defending what we believe in. We temper the military action by remembering that for the VN or VC [Viet Cong] death is the beginning. We can pray for those who die + for their families. God does not expect us to pray ≤ [with] same intensity or affection.

[Red]: No one blind or dear + therefore [3 dots] know that men hve [have] killed in cold blood ≤ [with]out any reason. What called? Murder. How justify? We can't. Looks at self in mirror—hope before they die they, in some way, express regret for it.

[Green]: Also—Prisoners. Force, not cruelty. Security, not sadism.

[Red]: Damage to self grtr thn dam. [greater than damage] to others.

Physical scar on other; open wound on self.

[Green]: This is not being naïve about the violence of war; nor is it a denial or over-simplification of conscience conflict war causes. IS a means of resolving problems ≤ [with]out betraying our conscience or being untrue to ourselves. 235

The Maryknoll Assistant Father General sent a letter in October to all Maryknoll priests serving with the military, asking their opinion about stipends. The Maryknoll practice was that the chaplain turned over his military salary to Maryknoll, and Maryknoll then sent a small stipend to the priest. Father Capodanno answered the questionnaire immediately, that the rule should be updated to allow the chaplain to use his military salary for the needs of his soldiers. He received the General Chapter's decisions by mid-November.236 Not only did the

---

235 NAV/Cap, Capodanno Files. N.p., n.d. Father Vincent R. Capodanno, MM, sermon notes.

236 MFBA, Box: Capodanno Personnel Files. Folder: Capodanno, Rev. Vincent R/Documents, N.p. November 13, 1966, "Assistant General" to Father Vincent R. Capodanno, MM.

General Chapter receive Father Capodanno's suggestions, but adopted them as a practical updating of the 1956 Rules and Regulations of the Society. The letter concluded with a postscript: "If you have any further suggestions that would be helpful, we would appreciate hearing from you."[237]

Father Capodanno was again with his Marines in the field during the final operation of November, Operation Rio Blanco/ Lien Ket 70. This was the final search and destroy mission of the 1/7 in conjunction with the Army of the Republic of Vietnam (ARVN) in the Quang Ngai Province, during the days and nights of November 20-27, 1966.

In a letter to his brother Albert and his wife Kathleen, Father Vincent briefly mentioned the operation, but nothing of the battles, lest his family worry about his safety:

> We spent Thanksgiving [Day] out in the field on an operation. By the way, I have heard that one of the RV Newscasts had a few minutes showing one of our Company's [sic] during the operation which was called Rio Blanca [sic]. Anyone happen to see it? Many amusing things turn up here but I think this one is tops: Thanksgiving evening I was walking around talking to the men as they (and I) ate C-rats [C-Rations: military issued canned food]. One young fellow called me over and showed me a humorous Thanksgiving card he had just received (mail is brought out by heliocopter [sic] . . . sometimes). He was sitting in the mud, soaking wet with a limited array of unpalatable C-rats in front of him as he read me part of the message: 'I have heard on the radio and seen on TV all about the wonderful turkey dinner all the men in Viet Nam are going to have on Thanksgiving Day. I bet your turkey dinner will be even better than

[237] MFBA, Box; Capodanno Personnel Files. Folder: Capodanno, Rev. Vincent R/Documents. N.p., November 13, 1966, "Assistant General" to Father Vincent R. Capodanno, MM.

ours at home.' He just looked stunned but four of us stood around and laughed for about five minutes.

I remember everyone at Mass; keep me in your own prayers.

God bless you, Vin.[238]

A more in-depth version of Father Capodanno's battlefield ministry was told by the Marines themselves in May, 1967, when Father Capodanno was awarded the Bronze Star by the President of the United States for his role with the First Battalion, Seventh Marines during the period of May 1, 1966 to December 9, 1966, in Operations Mobile, Franklin, Fresno, Golden Fleece 7-1, and Rio Blanco. The recommendations by Marines who served with him on the battlefields outline the essence of Father Capodanno's priestly ministry during his first eight months in Vietnam.

In his recommendation, Marine Major E.F. Fitzgerald wrote about Father Capodanno's priestly ministry, both in camp and on the battlefield. It is worth quoting him at length:

His [Father Capodanno's] conduct under fire was notably courageous and that of a very brave man. On numerous occasions this officer was observed running across exposed [rice] paddies and areas to be at the side of a Marine. With no apparent regard for his personal safety, thinking only of the wounded or dead Marine, he carried his inspiration and prayer to those who needed his help. Father CAPODANNO was particularly adept in putting men in the proper frame of mind before and during battle. He had the confidence and deep respect of the men and healed the scars which the loss of a friend frequently caused in those who survive. He eliminated bitterness from their hearts and instilled Christian

---

[238] AMIL, Box: Capodanno Correspondence Binder. N.p. December 4, 1966, Father Vincent R. Capodanno, MM, to Albert and Kathleen Capodanno.

determination and morals to be drawn against in future battle. He encouraged the men of all faiths to do more for their God, our Country, their Corps and themselves.

Few men have seen more combat action than their Chaplain. Invariably, he sought out that unit which was most likely to encounter the heaviest contact. He would then go with that unit and continually circulated along the route of march. During breaks, never resting, he moved among the men. His bravery, his humor, his right word at the right time contributed to the success of the unit.

He was particularly adept in observing a Marine who was troubled by the press of events and/or personal problems and who needed help and encouragement. He would share his rations, and his cigarettes as he quietly shared his thoughts with these men. Troubles seemed to disappear. Men found themselves after these informal sessions with this chaplain.

While in the battalion combat base he worked long hours. He established a library, wrote hundreds of letters to parents, and counseled the troops. He was firm and fair. When convinced a Marine needed help he spared no energy and left no stone unturned in assisting him. But through his influence men accepted their responsibilities. He instilled proper attitudes in the minds of the men toward the Vietnamese, and toward each other.

He always worked long into the night after his later hour visitors had departed his office. During the day he visited the outlying company bases and hospitals to offer prayer and revisit those with whom he had walked into combat. Frequently he went on small unit patrols. More than one young NCO [non-commissioned officer] patterned himself upon the examples of leadership and bravery set by Chaplain CAPODANNO.

At Christmas he gathered gifts from friends and

organizations all over the world to insure that no man in the Battalion was forgotten. He spent his own money to give his men items not readily available to them. On one occasion I witnessed Father CAPODANNO remove his rain suit and give it to a wounded Marine. For the remainder of the operation he was without suitable rain clothing.

This man was an inspiration to all who observed and served with him. He was known and loved throughout the Regiment. Weather and adverse conditions did not prevent him from visiting other organizations to offer services and to lead his men in prayer. [239]

Submitting testimony for the same Bronze Star commendation process, First Sergeant William L. DeLoach, USMC recalled:

He [Father Capodanno] was constantly seeking ways to make the trials of war a little more liveable [sic] for the men.

During monsoon seasons, Father continued to visit the companies of this battalion, even though the roads were almost impassable.

Regardless of race, religion, creed or color, Father Capodanno was always available to listen to the smallest or the largest problems of all Marines and each of their problems were [sic] of the deepest concern to him.[240]

Captain David L. Walker, USMC, remembered:

Father Capodanno was the first at my side, even though he had run about 75 meters through heavy enemy small arms fire. After summoning a Corpsman he then assisted

---

[239] CAP/Staten, Headquarters 7th Marines, San Francisco, May 26, 1967, Major E. F. Fitzgerald 058208 USMC to Commanding General, Fleet Marine Force, Pacific, pp. 2-3.

[240] CAP/Staten, N.p., n.d., 1st Sergeant William L. DeLoach, USMC.

in carrying me to a safe area where I was med-evaced. During this time he was constantly exposed to enemy fire.[241]

Captain Kenneth W. Johnson recalled, "He [Father Capodanno] repeatedly and purposely presented himself in those situations considered most difficult and dangerous, so that he might be instantly responsive to the needs of the Marines."[242]

Lieutenant Basil Lubka, who served with Father Capodanno, offered his recommendation:

> In truth, he was the 'Padre.' This was not a perfunctory title, but rather a reflection of the significant respect all hands had for him. This respect was earned by his total and complete willingness to share at all times the risks and privations of all members of the command. He suffered when the men suffered. He was their 'Rock of Ages.' Of his own volition, on operations, he deployed with the assault companies because he knew his services would be most needed by them. Within the TAOR [Tactical Area of Responsibility], he spent more days and nights at company combat bases than within the battalion CB [Command Base]. No problem was too small for him. All hands sought actively his sage counsel.[243]

Marine Lieutenant General Y.B. Krulak added his own commendation:

> In addition to his performance of duty on the battlefield, Chaplain CAPODANNO served as an example, and loyal friend to the officers and men of the Battalion. He worked long into the night to counsel and serve the men, to write to their parents and to assist them with

---

[241] CAP/Staten, N.p., May 15, 1967, Captain David L. Walker, USMC.

[242] CAP/Staten, N.p., May 20, 1967, Captain Kenneth W. Johnson, USMC.

[243] CAP/Staten, Headquarters, Chu Lai Installation, N.d., Lieutenant Basil Lubka, USMC.

their problems.

His fair, but firm, approach to the problems common to a combat area won the deep respect of the men.

By his example he instilled bravery and self-respect in his troops. He taught them to be Christians and men in face of the enemy and in their every day encounters with each other and with the Vietnamese.[244]

Father Capodanno never told his family, friends or fellow priests of this commendation and medal awarded him by the President of the United States. In his Christmas form letter, he mentioned none of this, sketching a picture of tranquil life in Vietnam, that was ". . . familiar to me because of Taiwan, even though the living standard here is considerably lower than in similar areas of Taiwan."[245] He reported that being the only Catholic chaplain in the entire 7th Marines kept him busy. He closed with instructions for sending gift packages to troops, asking prayers for the Marines:

I shall remember you all at Christmas. For many men here, it will be their first Christmas away from home; for many others, it will be their first Christmas in a combat zone. Please keep them all in your prayers on Christmas Day. . . they are a great group of men.

As Christmas approached, Father Capodanno informed his family in a hastily handwritten note that:

I was moved from 1/7 to the 1st Medical Bn. [Battalion] + am now the Catholic Chaplain at the Marines' Hospital here in Chu Lai. I moved here last Friday [December 9th] + have spent the past week getting organized + visiting the

---

[244] CAP/Staten, Headquarters, N.d., Lieutenant General Y.B. Krulak, USMC.

[245] AMIL, Box: Correspondence Binder. Chu Lai, South Viet Nam, November, 1966, Father Vincent R. Capodanno, MM, Christmas Form Letter.

men who are here as patients.[246]

Besides attending to the wounded and dying Marines, Father Capodanno also wrote their families. This was exceptionally important to keep families of injured soldiers informed of their sons' condition, especially as Christmas approached.

In a handwritten note, Father Capodanno informed the family of one of his Marines, Russ Sherrick, that he was writing the note as he sat alongside their son, who entered the hospital in the afternoon of Sunday, December 4, 1966. He assured the family that "He is doing exceptionally well. There is a cast on his right arm but that will be coming off soon. The damage to both the bone + nerve are [sic] TEMPORARY only. Russ can move + feel with all his fingers + the pins-and-needles sensation will diminish each day." He told the family their son would soon be moved to the Philippines, as were most soldiers after surgery, because the climate there "was more conducive to quick healing." He continued, "I can indeed understand your concern + worry, Mr. + Mrs. Sherrick, but Russ is really fine + his complete recovery is unquestionable." He closed by promising his prayers for them and for Russ, writing: "Our Christmas will be a fine one + I wish you all the blessings of this Holy Season."[247]

His final battlefield ministry of 1966 was in December, when Operation DeSoto began, the last major battle for Marine units in Quang Ngai Province, which would continue through the first months of the New Year. In his statement supporting the commendation of the priest chaplain for the Bronze Star, the commanding officer of Company M of the 3/7 reported Father Capodanno's heroism and dedication to the Marines of M Company under fire during Operation DeSoto:

[246] CAP/Staten, N.p., December 15, 1966, Father Vincent R. Capodanno, MM, to "Dear Dot + Tony".

[247] AMIL, Box: Correspondence Binder. N.p., December 10, 1966, Father Vincent R. Capodanno, MM, to Mr. & Mrs. Sherrick + Betty.

He repeatedly and purposely presented himself in these situations considered most difficult and dangerous, so that he might be instantly responsive to the needs of the Marines. His courage and valiant example has [sic] always been a source of strength to Marines of Company M, 3rd Battalion, 7th Marines. [248]

After Father Capodanno's death, one Marine's mother wrote the Capodanno Family:

On December 10th [1966] our son was wounded and taken to that hospital. Father was with him almost every hour of the two days our son was there before being sent to Clark Air Base. Father helped our son write me a letter (his last) telling us of his wounds. We were so thankful someone, who knew our Ray quite well, was with him his last few days of life on this earth. As you know it isn't easy to lose a loved one over 10,000 miles from you. Father wrote us several letters after our son's death which will always be a treasure to us. . . .

He wrote us, he hoped to meet us someday, I feel we have always known him, even though we never met. [249]

Reflecting on Operation DeSoto, Father Capodanno wrote to a correspondent friend back in the United States,

I think I understand now the origin of the pagans' worship of the Earth Mother: it must have begun when a man saw his friends' blood soaked up by foreign soil. Our casualties were really light but the circumstances

---

[248] CAP/Staten, N.p., May 20, 1967, Statement of Captain Kenneth W. Johnson 080872/0302 USMC.

[249] CAP/Staten, Carsonville, MI, January 14, 1968, Margie Herrington to Michael Capodanno "and all of Fr. Vincent Capodanno's Family."

left everyone breathing a bit quickly. [250]

His most impressive accomplishments were those imitating Our Lord. A Navy doctor working in the 1st Medical Battalion with Father Capodanno, Lieutenant Joseph L. LaHood recalled the compassion of their chaplain:

> But, never had I ever seen such dedication and selflessness, not as a sticky 'piety' but as a 'way.' For the hundreds of cigarettes he held for the wounded, many of whom could no longer reach their hands to their lips, and for the hundreds of letters he wrote and helped to write for his men, the Marines will never forget that he was one of them, this priest of God, is a hero.

> There was no question among all of us that God had endowed this man with a unique compassion, insight, and humility. What an example he was to the fighting men he served; how subtly he indicated, without words, that Christ was there! He was a legend. [251]

The legend was real and human, that of a very dedicated priest, with very basic concerns motivated by charitable concern for his Marines. Father Capodanno expressed his gratitude to his own family and friends in the United States, thanking them for remembering his Marines at Christmas:

> . . . your response to my request for packages and mail was indeed overwhelming. Our men here enjoyed immensely all the goodies you sent and were most pleased and happy that so many people thought of them during the Holidays. The packages, the cards, notes and letters really gave everyone's morale a boost.

---

[250] CAP/Staten, N.p., January 26, 1967, Father Vincent R. Capodanno, MM, to Clifford J. Laube.
[251] Quoted in Mode, *The Grunt Padre*, p. 101-102.

It was most kind of you all, and I, as well as all the men, thank you for your generosity. [252]

---

[252] CAP/Staten, South Vietnam, Spring, 1967, Father Vincent R. Capodanno, MM, Easter Form Letter, "Greetings and Gratitude from Chu Lai."

Chapter VI

Vietnam, 1967

As the United States became more deeply involved in the Vietnam War, so too did the attention of the world press, and the Battalion headquarters of the 7th Marines frequently played host to reporters. As seen above, Father Capodanno became one of the officers often interviewed, and he continued his association with some correspondents, even developing friendships he thought would last beyond Vietnam.

One such was the American Catholic reporter and poet, Clifford J. Laube. Father Capodanno wrote him after the New Year:

> Cliff, both your article and your letter are exceedingly complimentary and though while I am certain with an absolute certainty that I do not come close to your opinion of me, it is nice to know you think so highly of me. Perhaps I should hope that we do not meet again lest you become disillusioned. Nevertheless, I know you can cope with reality, so, come what may, I do hope our paths cross again.[253]

Laube had recently married, and Father Capodanno offered a brief meditation on Christian marriage:

> Marriage is a beautiful human experience and the marriage of two Christians has a beauty that is deep and magnificent beyond comparison. St. Paul went so far, and correctly so, to declare it the image of the union between Christ and the Church. Its love, and the inevitable sacrifice implied, are not simply profound in the conventional sense, but profound to the point of touching upon eachother's [sic] existence and purpose of life. Its full appreciation requires a sensitivity you already possess.

---

[253] CAP/Staten, N.p., January 26, 1967, Father Vincent R. Capodanno, MM, to "Dear Cliff."

Most sincerely I pray for your continued and mutual growth in eachother's [sic] love and through that love, your growth in the love of God.

On January 4, 1967, Father Capodanno submitted his request for an extension of overseas duty, and a "special thirty days leave".[254] His first tour of duty in Vietnam would end in April, and, while not impossible, a request for an extension of duty by a chaplain was rarely granted. Usually, following a chaplain's tour of duty, he would be assigned a billet in the United States, after which the chaplain could request another assignment. Father Capodanno informed his superiors that his stateside address would be that of his sister and brother-in-law, Pauline and George Costa. He wrote his family the news on January 20th:

> Yours came recently while I was in Hong Kong for R & R [Rest and Relaxation]. I returned last night (left last Friday). I went with a Major who was out at 1/7 while I was there. Both he and I have been transferred but get together now and then. He was real good company and we had a real good time together. I looked up the Maryknollers there and we were able to get together several times for dinner.

> Just before going to HK [Hong Kong] I put in my request to extend my tour here for six months. When I returned last evening I found out it was accepted. I will get leave and then return. Tentatively, I will leave here in late April and be due back in late May. I am planning to make a few stops along the way so all in all I should have about two weeks with y'all. I have no idea when I'll be there and won't have any idea for along [sic] time. I'll let you know as soon as I can.

---

[254] AMIL, Box: Capodanno Official Record 1. San Francisco, January 4, 1967, Lieutenant Vincent R. Capodanno to Commanding General, 1st Marine Division (Rein), FMF.

I remember everyone at Mass. Keep us all in your prayers.[255]

Just a few days after writing, on January 26, 1967, Operation DeSoto resumed, the last major battle for the Marine units in the Quang Ngai Province. Father Capodanno kept brief notes in his pocket diary describing some of the military operations. Usually, the diaries simply provided paper for his hurried scribbling of soldiers' names, their families, and duties to be performed, that bore no relationship to the printed date of the diary. For example, while the year printed on the diary cover is 1966, his entries actually refer to events of 1967. This is seen by context, names and places. He arrived in Vietnam after Easter, 1966, so the entries are dated for months he saw only once in Vietnam, during 1967. He used the calendar pages dated 1966 to record events and information of battles of 1967.

For instance, on an end paper of the 1966 diary, he made notes about a young Marine, wounded on February 18, 1967: "2/18—hot evaced [evacuated] because of fire fight. Walked into C+C—bed for 10 days. Shrapnel in stomach from airstrike mis-fire. Parents contacted, notified as a result of hostile action. Written up by XO [Executive Officer] for Pur[ple] Heart."[256] While the printed date is February, 1966, the events are those of February, 1967, since Father Capodanno was not in Vietnam in February, 1966.

Under the dates, January 10-16, 1966, he recorded notes for a sermon, possibly for a funeral or memorial service. Father Capodanno was not in Vietnam in January, 1966. It would seem more probable that he penned these for a sermon appropriate for the sufferings of his Marines during the January and February days of the 1967 Operation DeSoto:

---

[255] CAP/Staten, N.p., January 20, 1967, Father Vincent R. Capodanno, MM, to Lydia and James Capodanno.

[256] AMIL, Box: Correspondence Binder. *Featherweight Diary, 1966*, Lt. Vincent Capodanno, endpaper.

At an event such as this, willingly or no, consciously or no, our minds grope amid the tragedies + complexities of life looking for an answer. It is with hesitation that we accept the fact: there is no easy answer, there is no glib answer. We are human beings + our view + nolege [knowledge] are ltd [limited] because of our human limitations. We grdly [gradually] realize we must face these events with Faith in God. Knowing that somehow these events have a meaning that somehow they work for the good of the persons involved. We cannot fully comprehend how but only that they do. [257]

On the pages for the dates May 13-19, 1966, Father Capodanno scrawled his notes about another incident he was involved in on February 22, 1967, during Operation DeSoto:

Feb 22 at 15:00 in Min[h] Lon[g] Area S.F. (3) c̲ 170 CIDG [Civilian Irregular Defense Group] men coming down from Hill 1047 to evacuate wounded 17-108 (S.F. [Special Forces] same unit of Americans) among whom was Sgt. Bodlak. Terrain made chopper loading impossible. Plateau (rice paddies) chopper cldnt [couldn't] get out. Wounded unloaded. Sniper fire all the time—small arms + automatic. Adge [Air Defence Ground Environment] crossed stream to ascend Hill 793 + have chopper land on top saddle. All CIDG made it across. Capt hit— . . . took him up hill. M/Sgt. [Master Sergeant] Sanchez + Sgt. Jaroslav BODLAK at base in stream giving cover fire as Capt. ascended. Airstikes coming in. Sanchez took Sgt + dragged him to top of hill. Mont guards + SF [Special Forces] men assisted until chopper came at 22:30. [258]

---

[257] AMIL, Box: Correspondence Binder. *Featherweight Diary, 1966*, Lt. Vincent Capodanno, January 10-16.

[258] AMIL, Box: Correspondence Binder. *Featherweight Diary, 1966*, Lt. Vincent Capodanno, pp. May 13-May 19.

Under April 29-May 1st can be found this entry about a young Marine:

> Blast injury on left wrist, loss of muscle + tendons in forearm. Has damage in left leg—calf injury. 2 or 3 small pieces of shrap[nel] in face near left eye. Mike Braswell, Birmingham, Alabama. [259]

Father Capodanno wrote frequently to family members of young Marines, sometimes requesting supplies for the men, or, more frequently, informing families of injuries sustained in battle or of death on the battlefield. Here are some examples:

> John Farabee — Delta [Company]; mail 6 packages of Boots + Socks.

> Daryl Larson — Delta; cf. Cpl. [Corporal] Schaeffer (2nd PLT [Platoon]), check on personal effects + mail.

> Tom Fuqua — 2258768, Only son — what arrangement for being in Vietnam?

> Cpl. Lenyszyn, B.M. [Boatswain's mate], Min Lon, 2133139, Symptoms of Malaria. Evac, 10 Oct. [260]

After Father Capodanno's death on the battlefield, the family of a young Marine who received the Last Rites from Father Capodanno, remembered: "Altho [sic] he had little time for himself he took time out to write to the parents of a young boy he had administered the Last Rites to in Viet Nam last year, L/Cpl. [Lance Corporal] Thomas Tamilio, our nephew."[261]

By March, Father Capodanno provided additional details of his upcoming leave to his brother James Capodanno and his

---

[259] AMIL, Box: Correspondence Binder. *Featherweight Diary, 1966*, Lt. Vincent Capodanno, pp. April 29-May 1.

[260] AMIL, Box: Correspondence Binder. *Featherweight Diary, 1966*, Lt. Vincent Capodanno, pp. December 9-10; December 31.

[261] AMIL, Box: Correspondence Binder. Yonkers, February 14, 1968, Mr. & Mrs. R.W. Dietrich to Mrs. Costa.

wife, Lydia. He planned to go to Manila for retreat at the end of April, return to Chu Lai and then begin his leave, spending a few days visiting friends in Taipei, Tokyo and Honolulu, and then return to his family. "Including travel time (which includes waiting for military planes) it will be sometime in the middle of May before I am actually back in the U.S."[262]

His leave was delayed, however, because of "Temporary Additional Duty," which began a thirty day extension of duty with the 1st Marine Hospital Company "on or about 9 May 1967."[263] Two days later, he was informed that he had received two further military decorations for his service: The National Defense Medal, and The Vietnam Defense Medal with Fleet Marine Force Combat Operations Insignia and one 3/16-inch bronze star.[264]

As he waited for his leave, he continued his ministry to the wounded, as a young Marine, James L. Taylor, recalled years later:

> Father Vincent touched me in such a way, and I know for a fact others, I will never forget him. I first meet [sic] him in Da Nang Hospital. I caught a sniper round in my ancle [sic] and about 3 AM or 4 AM he came in. Everyone else was asleep but I was in such pain and I could not sleep. I remember it like it was yesterday he walked in walked over to me + sat beside me. He introduced himself + said your [sic] in a lot of pain aren't you, and of course my reply was yes sir. He held my hand + we talked for a few minutes about where I was from + were [sic] he was from and then he made the sign of the

---

[262] CAP/Staten, N.p., March 29, 1967, Father Vincent R. Capodanno, MM, to Lydia and James Capodanno.

[263] AMIL, Box: Capodanno Official Records 2, San Francisco, May 9, 1967, R. L. Grice by direction of the Commanding Officer to Lieutenant Vincent R. Capodanno.

[264] CAP/Staten, Headquarter 1st Medical Battalion, San Francisco, May 11, 1967, J.M. Robertson by direction of Commanding Officer to Lieutenant Vincent R. Capodanno, CHC, USNR, 656197/4105.

Cross and touched my ancle [sic], and James as god [sic] as [sic] my witness the pain competly [sic] went away, I could not believe it. He said you rest now + in the morning after chow come + help me at the chapel [sic]. So I did. I worked him [sic] for there [sic] for about 5 days. Until I was ready to go back into combat.

Before I left he gave me a St. Christifer [sic] metal [sic] on the back its [sic] says Viet Nam 67. I still have it.

James, I'm telling you for the 4-5 years after that, there wasn't a day that went buy [sic] that I didn't think about him. He touched me so much. [265]

Father Capodanno finally arrived home by the end of May, and stayed with his sister Pauline and her family in Kearny, New Jersey. During this brief visit home, his family recognized that the young priest they sent to the missions of Taiwan had returned a changed man. His brother James recalled:

"It was the first time I saw a change in Vincent. He had changed tremendously. His hair was gray. He would be sitting right across from us, but his mind was in Vietnam. He couldn't wait until he got back to Vietnam."[266]

A telegram dated June 6, 1967 cut short Father Capodanno's visit with his family:

"Your special 30 day leave orders are modified. Report to the Marine Liaison Building 678, MAC [Military Assistance Command] Terminal, Norton Air Force Base, San Bernardino, California not later than 0900 9 JUN67."[267]

Father Capodanno arrived in Danang, Vietnam on June 7,

---

[265] CAP/Staten, Moorpark, CA, September 7, 1996, James L. Taylor to James Capodanno.

[266] Quoted in Mode, *The Grunt Padre*, p. 108.

[267] AMIL, Box: Capodanno Official Records 1. WESTERN UNION, San Francisco, June 6, 1967, "MARBKS MAYSTA SFRAN" to Lieutenant Vincent R. Capodanno.

1967. He wrote his sister Pauline the following day:

> I am going, eventually, to the 1st Battalion, 5th Marines. For the next three weeks or so, I am going to be filling in for two priests who are going on Retreat. I'll be here for ten days at the hospital where I was before returning to the States, + then go, also for ten days, to my old unit, 1st Bn [Battalion], 7th Mar. [Marines] sometime around 1 July I will go to the 1st Bn [Battalion], 5th Mar.[268]

The formal orders were dated June 10th, and effective July 3rd.[269] He wrote his family later that month, "All is well here at 1/7. It is good seeing everyone again, especially since many will soon be leaving and also the fact that I didn't expect to get to be around 1/7 at all makes this brief stay with them that much nicer."[270] He then told them, "When I move to 1/5, I will be about half-way back down to Chu Lai and about half-way away from Danang. The general area is called Tam Ky. I don't think it appears on any maps used by newspapers."

Upon arriving at the 1st Battalion, 5th Marine command post, Father Capodanno reported to the battalion commander, Colonel Peter Hilgartner. He was assigned as chaplain to the entire 5th Regiment, and decided to extend his priestly ministry beyond the command post by accompanying Colonel Hilgartner on his nightly patrols to the outlying defense posts that protected the Battalion headquarters from night attacks by the North Vietnamese Army [NVA]. Father Capodanno was the first chaplain to "walk the lines" to be with the Marines exposed to hostile night attacks.

On July 10, 1967, Father Capodanno submitted his

---

[268] AMIL, Box: Correspondence Binder. N.p. June 8, 1967, Father Vincent R. Capodanno, MM, to Pauline + George.

[269] CAP/Staten, San Francisco, June 10, 1967, "Division Special Order number 427-67."

[270] AMIL, Box: Correspondence Binder. N.p. June 27, 1967, Father Vincent R. Capodanno, MM, to Pauline + George.

paperwork for a six month extension of his overseas tour of duty in Vietnam, further requesting that he be permitted to remain with the 1st Marine Division. The reason for his request was simply expressed: "I do not wish to leave."[271] His request was endorsed by D.L. McIngturff, Commanding Officer, H & S Companies 1st Battalion, 5th Marines; P.L. Hilgartner, Commanding Officer, 1st Battalion, 5th Marines, and by A.N. Kendrick, Commanding General, 1st Marine Division.

Despite the high-ranking endorsements, his request for a second extension of duty in Vietnam was denied on August 2nd, because he was needed elsewhere. The Chief of Chaplains wrote him: "The experience and knowledge which you have obtained are needed in other assignments. It is equally important that as many chaplains in our corps as possible have an opportunity to serve in Vietnam."[272] He was needed in Newport, Rhode Island to train new, young chaplains who would replace him on the battlefield.

Father Capodanno determined to apply once again, this time for a mere two month extension of duty. [273] His repeated requests for extended tours of duty in Vietnam were all denied. "I even offered to forfeit my 30-day rest-and-recreation leave in order to be with the boys at Christmas. . . . So, it looks like one way or another, I'll be out of the Orient by December."[274]

Even while his requests were denied, Father Capodanno continued to work for his Marines. In his final form letter to his family and friends, Father Capodanno sent further instructions home about what could be sent to his Marines. He suggested

---

[271] CAP/Staten, N.p., July 10, 1967, Memorandum: Lieutenant Vincent R. Capodanno to Commanding General, 1st Marine Division (Rein), FMF.

[272] CAP/Staten, N.p., MEMORANDUM, August 2, 1967, James W. Kelly to Lieutenant Vincent R. Capodanno.

[273] CAP/Staten, N.p., August 25, 1967, Father Vincent R. Capodanno, MM, to Lydia, James and Jim Capodanno.

[274] CAP/Staten, N.p., August 27, 1967, Father Vincent R. Capodanno, MM, to Albert Capodanno.

"Any goodies" and what he called "space blankets," which he described as ". . . blanket-shaped, water-proof, heat-proof, cold-proof, light-weight, costs about 8 or 9 dollars and is probably sold in some camping or sports goods stores."[275]

As Captain David J. Casazza recalled, Father Capodanno preferred to be closer to transportation so he could visit the troops, and asked to be moved:

> He was bothered by the lack of transportation and the difficulty and loss of time encountered in getting to the other Battalions of the 5th Marines. So, shortly before I left I transferred him to 3/5, --located at Regimental Headquarters. There the Regimental Commander's helo [helicopter] was available to him so he could spend more time with his men. [276]

By mid-August, Father Capodanno received his transfer from the 1st Battalion to the 3rd Battalion, 5th Marines, which provided him easier access to all three battalions and to the regimental headquarters.

Another recollection of Father Capodanno's insistence to have ready access to his Marines of 3/5 was relayed to a School Sister of Notre Dame by a Navy doctor, Joseph E. Pilon, who had served with Father Capodanno:

> We had a chaplain, a Maryknoll priest by the name of Capodanno who had been over here for 16 months. Usual tour of duty in Vietnam is 12 months but the good padre had it extended on the condition that he would be allowed to continue with the 'grunts'. He wasn't a young man. . . but he appeared, in spite of his quiet, unpretentious manner, to be a veritable thorn in the

---

[275] CAP/Staten, N.p. Summer, 1967, Father Vincent R. Capodanno, MM, Form Letter.

[276] AMIL, Box: Funeral Binder. Newport, RI, February 5, 1968, Captain David J. Casazza, CHC, USN, "Memorial Remarks at the Dedication of the Capodanno Chapel," p. 2.

Division Chaplain's bald head. The D.C. wanted Fr. C. to live at Division Headquarters from which he could 'spoke' out to all the battalions in the division—but Fr. C. would have none of that. His mission was to the grunts—to the boys fighting in the front lines whom he felt really needed the chaplain. He refused to play the percentages that he would be able to get to more people in the rear areas.

His audience was always a small group of 20-40 Marines gathered together on a hillside, or behind some rocks, hearing confessions—saying Mass. It was almost as though he had decided to leave the 'other 99 in a safe area and go after the one who had gotten in trouble. [277]

Lieutenant Commander Eli Takesian, a close friend of Father Capodanno and the Presbyterian minister and chaplain to the 5th Marines, recalled the first time he saw Father Capodanno as he was offering Mass for the 3/5 Marines in his tent. Commander Takesian recalled, "It [the Mass] was almost like seeing a ballet—the utter grace, sureness. It was mesmerizing."[278] The Mass was an essential part of Father Capodanno's ministry to the Marines.

Chaplain Charles T. Kelly wrote about Father Capodanno in his "End of Tour Report" in late September, 1967:

Following Father Capodanno was like attending a class in what a good chaplain should do. He knew every man by his name and all knew him. He never said much but people remembered what he said. He was with his Marines in the field, in the club, in the mess hall. I don't think he ever intended to leave them.[279]

---

[277] AMIL, Box: Funeral Binder. Mt. Calvary, Wisconsin, January 8, 1969, Sister George Marie, SSND to "Dear Father."

[278] Quoted in Mode, *The Grunt Padre*, p. 114.

[279] AMIL, Box: Medal of Honor Support. N.p., n.d., Chaplain Charles T. Kelly, "End of Tour Report," p. 4.

Lieutenant Frederick Smith remembered Father Vincent:

> He was a unique man. . . he just had a personality and a demeanor which enlisted a great deal of affection and respect and almost instantaneously. I never knew anybody who had anything but the highest regard for Father Capodanno. He was a man who had the courage of a lion and the faith of a martyr. [280]

One of the Navy Corpsmen working with Father Capodanno at 3/5, described working with the chaplain to the Capodanno family:

> I've thought of his family often over the years, and hoped that they understood the love that he had for 'his Marines'. As a Combat Corpsman, this was something your Brother and I shared. Many a time we divided up the body and the soul of an errant Marine, and put forth our best efforts to get him back on track. [281]

The former Corpsman then related the details of Father Capodanno's and his efforts to help a young Marine at 3/5, during August, 1967. The Marine had asked his 1st Sergeant for permission to return home to settle a disagreement with his girlfriend. His 1st Sergeant denied his request, and one night the Marine became intoxicated and vowed vengeance. The Marine returned and ran into Corpsman Perez, who continued the story:

> Not knowing his intentions, and all Marines during that time walked round fully loaded, and armed to the teeth, I first stripped the bolt from his weapon, disarming it, before any discussions occurred. With the bolt safely in my pocket, a very tearful and confused Marine confessed to me that for the last hour he had been lying in wait, up where the 1st Sgt. had his tent, waiting for him to show up,

---

[280] Quoted in Mode, *The Grunt Padre*, p. 112.

[281] CAP/Staten, Juneau, Alaska, November 14, 1996, Vic "Doc" Perez to James Capodanno.

so he could kill him. There are times when a Marine tends to confuse a Corpsman with a Chaplain, and this was definitely one of those times. After I felt that I had correctly assessed the situation, prompted by the fact that there was still beer that needed drinking, I and the Marine in tow, went in search for the Padre. I knew by past experience, that Father Capodanno would normally be in his tent at that hour, either writing letters, or reading.

True to his character, the Padre treated this intrusion as an opportunity to assist one of his Marines, any clime, any time. I used the side of the Padre's tent to support the Marine, braced by his rifle, and went on to explain what the problem was. When I got to the part about the 1st Sgt., and the Marine's intentions, I knew I had the good Father's utmost attention. We both came to a quick agreement that it was not soul saving, prayer, or preaching that was needed, but an understanding ear, followed up with a stern 'Father to Son' type talk. The Padre assured me that he was up to the challenge, and I was now free to return to reducing the supply of beer available to our rag tag organization.

Just as it appeared that Father Capodanno had worked out how to get our Marine unjammed [sic] off the side of his tent, I pulled out the bolt of his rifle from my pocket, and said, 'Oh, by the way, . . . it seemed like a good idea at the time that I should disarm him, considering circumstances. . . . Feel free to give it back to him when you're through!' I honestly believe that this was the only time that I had ever witnessed a stutter from the good Father.

Once settled into his new assignment at 3/5, among his many duties and good works Father Capodanno ordered simple religious medals for his Marines: on one side of the medal was Saint Christopher carrying the infant Christ, and on the other side, *Vietnam 1967*. He regularly distributed Saint Christopher medals to the Marines during Masses for Mike Company, [282] to Marines in the hospital, and to those about to go into battle. [283]

Father Capodanno's final shipment of Saint Christopher medals arrived on Sunday, September 3rd, 1967, which he personally blessed that day. It was his intention to distribute one medal to every man in his Battalion as they prepared for Operation Swift, which would begin the next day, September 4, 1967. [284]

[282] AMIL, Box: Medal of Honor Support. San Francisco, February 7, 1968, Private First Class Julio Rodriquez to "The Family of Chaplain Vincent R. Capodanno, LT, USN.

[283] CAP/Staten, Moorpark, CA, September 7, 1996, James L. Taylor to James Capodanno.

[284] AMIL, Box: Funeral Binder. San Francisco, February 24, 1968, Chaplain Eli Takesian to Pauline Costa.

Chapter VII
September 4, 1967

The Que Song Valley runs along the border of Quang Nam and Quang Tin Provinces in Vietnam. In 1967, the Valley was both populous and rich in fertile rice paddies. The People's Army of Vietnam considered the control of the Valley essential and, so, infiltrated the area earlier in the year.

The 5th Marine Regiment had been deployed to Vietnam during the previous summer of 1966. They were assigned to the Valley in 1967 to support the forces of the South Vietnamese Army. During the late summer of 1967, the American forces worked to secure the Valley from further infiltration by North Vietnamese forces, and to protect the upcoming elections and the rice harvest.

Operation Swift was the last of the Marine operations in the Que Son Valley during 1967, and began unexpectedly on the morning of September 4th when Delta Company, 1st Battalion, 5th Marines, was attacked before dawn outside the village of Dong Son by the People's Army of Vietnam.

The commanding officer in the field, Lieutenant Colonel Peter Hilgartner, requested the assistance of two companies from the 3rd Battalion. The request was granted by the 3rd Battalion commanding officer, Lieutenant Colonel Charles B. Webster, who assigned both Mike and Kilo Companies of 3/5 to be transported by helicopters to reinforce Delta Company.[285]

Father Capodanno requested and then insisted that he be permitted to board an outbound helicopter from Headquarters to be with his men in the battlefield. Such insistence and permission were unheard of, and bespoke the devotion of the chaplain to the men of 3/5, and the serious nature of their battlefield situation. First Sergeant Richard L. Kline of "M"

---

[285] CAP/Staten, San Francisco, September 5, 1967, Father John S. Keeley to Force Chaplain, Fleet Marine Force, Pacific.

Company later recalled:

> Chaplain Capodanno had initially approached me about the possibility of going out on a Company Search and Destroy mission with Mike Company. I told him this was unheard of for a chaplain to go out with a Line Company, where he would be exposed to enemy small arms fire. I personally denied his request, to the extent that I did not even inform the Company Commander of the Chaplain's request. However, Chaplain Capodanno informed me that he would see the Battalion Commander for his approval. Evidently, this was approved somewhere along the line, because he did end up in Mike company operation in September, 1967. [286]

The helicopters left Headquarters by 10 a.m. Because of the heavy ground fire, the helicopters were forced to land four kilometers east-northeast of Dong Son, their original landing site.

Upon landing, Father Capodanno was with the command post of Company M, 3rd Battalion, 5th Marines, behind the Second Platoon. Before the troops began their march to Dong Son, Father Capodanno gave General Absolution and Holy Communion to those Catholic Marines who wished to receive. Corporal John Scafidi recalled the effect the Sacraments had on the Marines:

> The reason for our calm, cool, total business attitude was we were given General Absolution along with Communion by Chaplain Capodanno just as we first started to walk that morning. I remember seeing him giving Communion before to those who wanted it, but not the entire formation. [287]

After 12 noon, Companies "K" and "M" began their march.

---

[286] Quoted in Mode, *The Grunt Padre*, p. 126.
[287] Quoted in Mode, *The Grunt Padre*, p. 127-128.

Father Capodanno was proceeding in column with the Command Post of "M" Company, 3rd Battalion, 5th Marines, between the First and Second Platoons. As the First Platoon advanced to the base of the hill, suddenly, "all hell broke loose and the platoon was inundated with a heavy barrage of mortar and an automatic weapon onslaught. The attack was sudden and lethal. There was nowhere to turn. Their ranks were being decimated." [288] At the Command Post, Father Capodanno listened to the frantic radioman reporting the onslaught of his Marines: "We can't hold out here. We are being wiped out! There are wounded and dying all around." It was then that Father Capodanno left the relative protection of the Command Post and ran forward to the position of the Second Platoon, then under fire and retreating up the hill.

Private First Class Stephen A. Lovejoy of "M" Company, 3/5, was the first Marine Father Capodanno assisted. Private Lovejoy recalled:

> Chaplain CAPODANNO left the Command Post and ran under fire to the Second Platoon's position which was 75-100 meters away. I was operating my radio and received word to pull back and form a tight perimeter. As I was pulling back, heavy mortar and small arms fire was coming in. I was dragging my radio and as I hit the deck the Chaplain dropped beside me and helped me up and to safety behind a small knoll. Without his help, I am sure I would have lost my life. At this time a friendly [U.S. military] gas attack was launched. The Chaplain did not have his gas mask with him and he refused to accept one from anyone else, saying 'No you keep it, you need it more than I do'. He gave last rites and aid to the dead and wounded Marines while continually exposed to the deadly hail of enemy fire, without regard for his own

---

[288] AMIL, Box: Medal of Honor Support. Father Ernest Passero, SJ, "Marine Chaplain, Rev. Father Vincent R. Capodanno Medal of Honor Winner," p. 12. Unpublished account.

personal safety. [289]

Lance Corporal Lovejoy later repeated, "I would never have made it up that hillside alive, if it weren't for Father Capodanno."[290]

One of the Marines mentioned by Private Lovejoy who received the last rites from Father Capodanno was Lance Corporal Steven Cornell of "M" Company, Second Platoon. Corporal David Brooks witnessed a mortar shell burst near Father Capodanno, and reported that "His arm was then observed to be covered with shrapnel wounds and to be hanging limply at his side."[291] "He continued to move among the wounded giving last rites, assuring the dying that 'Jesus is the truth and the life'," recalled Second Lieutenant Edward Blecksmith. [292] Under heavy fire, the Chaplain then made his way across ground exposed to heavy gun fire to Sergeant Lawrence Peters, "M" Company, Second Platoon. The Sergeant was Russian Orthodox, and Father Capodanno prayed the "Our Father" with him before he died. [293] Lance Corporal David Brooks of "M" Company, Second Platoon, witnessed Father Capodanno:

> . . . running while under heavy automatic fire to aid wounded men trying to comfort them and on many Marines acting as a shield placing himself between the

---

[289] AMIL, Box: Medal of Honor Support. San Francisco, September 21, 1967, Memorandum: Chaplain Charles T. Kelly: "Death of Chaplain Vincent R. Capodanno, Chaplain 3rd Battalion, 5th Marines": Statement of Private First Class Stephen A. LOVEJOY, 2248516/0311 USMC Company "M," 3rd Battalion, 5th Marines, 1st Marine Division (Rein), FMF.

[290] AMIL, Box: Medal of Honor Support. N.p., n.d., Chaplain Charles T. Kelly, "End of Tour Report," p. 2.

[291] AMIL, Box: Medal of Honor Support. San Francisco, September 21, 1967, Memorandum: Chaplain Charles T. Kelly: "Death of Chaplain Vincent R. Capodanno, Chaplain 3rd Battalion, 5th Marines," p. 2r.

[292] AMIL, Ibid. "Statement of 2nd Lieutenant Edward I. BLECKSMITH 0100868, USMC "M" Company, 3rd Battalion, 5th Marines, 1st Marine Division (RIEN), FMF.

[293] AMIL, Box: Medal of Honor Support. N.p., n.d., Chaplain Charles T. Kelly, "End of Tour Report," p. 2.

automatic weapons and the wounded Marine without concern for his own safety. Even though he seemed to be hit himself, I witnessed him giving a wounded man assistance and heard the Chaplain say, 'Jesus said have Faith', and then proceeded on to other wounded Marines stopping by all wounded Marines in his path. The Chaplain's example of action and courage to everyone who observed him sparked other [sic] into action. Quite a few more people would have died if not for him. This was the last time that I saw the Chaplain alive. [294]

The next eye witness, Lance Corporal Keith J. Rounseville, reported:

I did not see Chaplain CAPODANNO during the first moments of intense fighting. When I did see him, he was jumping over my [fox] hole, all the while exposing himself to enemy machine gun fire to try and give aid to a wounded Marine [Sergeant Howard Manfra]. Chaplain CAPODANNO looked and acted cool and calm, as if there wasn't an enemy in sight. As he reached the wounded Marine, Chaplain CAPODANNO laid beside him and gave him aid and verbal encouragement and telling him medical help was on the way. At this time Chaplain CAPODANNO was in the direct line of an enemy machine gun position. I told the Chaplain to take cover, but he stayed, praying with the wounded Marine. My rifle had a malfunction and I yelled at the Chaplain, 'Father, my rifle doesn't work', his reply was, 'Here, take the Sergeant's rifle', and further exposing himself to get the rifle for me. He stayed with the wounded Marine a little longer comforting him. When I last saw the Chaplain, he was going outside our perimeter to try and help other wounded Marines.

---

[294] AMIL, Ibid. "Statement of Lance Corporal David BROOKS, 2145602, USMC "M" Company, 3rd Battalion, 5th Marines, 1st Marine Division (REIN), FMF.

Chaplain CAPODANNO inspired everyone that day as he valiantly and without regard for his own personal safety, caring only for the troops' well being went from one wounded Marine to another giving aid. [295]

Lance Corporal Frederick Tancke recalled that Father Capodanno:

> . . . immediately began administering medical aid to the Marines who were wounded in action and giving last rites to the Marines killed in action by the heavy mortar fire and small arms weapons fire. He was then wounded by shrapnel in the arms, hand, and legs, and refused medical attention. The corpsman tried to patch him together but he waved him off. He said he wanted the wounded Marines to be taken care of first. After helping the Marines on the top of the hill he then ran down toward where the North Vietnamese Army were [sic] attacking, helping everyone he could find. At that time I was beside a dying corpsman, [Armando G. Leal] dragging another corpsman up the hill away from the charging North Vietnamese Army which I could see coming up the hill. I was trying to stop the bleeding when I saw an enemy with a machine gun about 15 meters [sic—15 feet] away. I was shot in the finger and dived into a hole to return fire.

> When Chaplain CAPODANNO got about 40 meters [sic-40 feet] down the hill he stopped for a second. I said 'watch out, there's a Viet Cong with a machinegun.' The Viet Cong laughed at me, squatted down with his machinegun and stayed there. The Chaplain was crouched down in cover and seeing the [injured] corpsman, he jumped out from cover and ran over about

---

[295] AMIL, Ibid. San Francisco, September 21, 1967, Memorandum: Chaplain Charles T. Kelly: "Death of Chaplain Vincent R. Capodanno, Chaplain 3rd Battalion, 5th Marines": Statement of Lance Corporal Keith J. ROUNSEVILLE, 2235872 USMC "M" Company, 3rd Battalion, 5th Marines, 1st Marine Division (REIN), FMF.

20 feet to the corpsman, right to his side. I heard enemy machinegun fire and the Chaplain fell by the corpsman's side. He actually jumped out in front of a machinegun that the North Vietnamese Army set up about 15 meters [sic— 15 feet] from me and the wounded [Marine]. He [Father Capodanno] had begun to give medical attention to the corpsman and three or four wounded Marines when the machinegun opened up and killed him. I am sure he knew the Viet Cong machinegunner [sic] was there and was set up. The Viet Cong fired two bursts both of which hit near me, and one or both bursts hit the Chaplain. [296]

Private First Class Julio Rodriquez also witnessed the battlefield ministry of Father Capodanno from another vantage point on September 4th. He recalled that Mike Company divided into platoons,

Then the V.C. [Viet Cong] Snipers started hitting us. We went after the Snipers who were on a hill. As we got to the top of the hill, and started down the other side, we realized it was an ambush. By this time, the mortar rounds were coming in heavy. Intelligence reports indicated there were two battalions of N.V.A. [North Vietnamese Army]. We quickly set our perimeter defense. The N.V.A. started up the hill in human waves. They completely surrounded the hill. By this time half of my platoon was wounded or dead.

This is when I first spotted Father Capodanno. He was carrying a wounded Marine. After he brought him into the relative safety of our perimeter, he continued to go back and forth giving Last Rites to dying men and bringing in wounded Marines. He made many trips, telling us to 'stay cool; don't panic'. Father passed by my

---

[296] AMIL, Box: Medal of Honor Support. "Statement of Lance Corporal Frederick W. TANCKE, 2207054/0311 USMC Company "M," 3rd Battalion, 5th Marines, 1st Marine Division (REIN), FMF.

[fox] hole and we told him to get in. The V.C. were only 10-15 feet away. The one surviving corpsman [Armand G. Leal] was still outside helping men, when he was hit and killed. Father went out to get the Corpsman. While doing so, the N.V.A. came up the hill again and one V.C. jumped from behind a bush and shot Father from behind. He was killed instantly.[297]

The entire series of events involving Father Capodanno took place within approximately 30 minutes after he entered the battle on the afternoon of September 4, 1967. [298]

The United States Navy sent the Capodanno Family official notification by Western Union of Father Capodanno's death. [299]

Cardinal Spellman, as Vicar of the Military Ordinariate, made the final decision in favor of the Capodanno Family's preference to take charge of all burial arrangements for their brother. Father Vincent's brothers preferred to bury him in Arlington National Cemetery. But the five Capodanno sisters overruled them, [300] and took charge of the reception of the body, the funeral and burial arrangements, rather than allowing their brother to be buried either in Arlington National Cemetery or in the Maryknoll cemetery in Ossining, New York. [301]

One of Father Capodanno's brothers, who had been working as a civilian with a contracting company in Vietnam at

---

[297] AMIL, Box: Medal of Honor Support. San Francisco, February 7, 1968, Private First Class Julio Rodriquez to "The Family of Chaplain Vincent R. Capodanno, LT, USN."

[298] AMIL, Box Medal of Honor Support. N.p., n.d., [Private First Class] Stephen A. Lovejoy, "Corrections to Battlefield Eyewitness Accounts," p. 2: 20-2.

[299] CAP/Staten, Western Union Cable, Washington, D.C., September 8, 1967, 11:33 a.m., Vice Admiral BJ Semmes, Jr. to James Capodanno.

[300] AMIL, Box: Capodanno Personal Testimonies. Staten Island, January 28, 2014, Interview of Doctor Vincent Maligno by Monsignor Stephen M. DiGiovanni.

[301] CAP/Staten, Maryknoll, September 14, 1967, Very Reverend John J. McCormack, MM, to Most Reverend William J. Moran.

the time of Father Capodanno's death, accompanied the body home. [302] The remains of Father Capodanno arrived at the home of his sister Pauline and her family in Kearny, New Jersey on September 15th. It was there that the wake was held on September 16th and 17th. The funeral Mass was offered at Queen of Peace Church in North Arlington, New Jersey on Tuesday, September 19th, followed by burial with his parents in Saint Peter's Cemetery on Staten Island. [303]

In his eulogy delivered at the funeral Mass of Father Capodanno, Chaplain Eli Takesian spoke of his friend and fellow chaplain:

> Chaplain Vincent Robert Capodanno died in the manner in which he lived; unselfishly. He was ascetic, humble and thoughtful, a man imbued with the spirit of Christ.

> Eyewitnesses to Chaplain Capodanno's death said that as elements of 'Mike' Company were being overrun, Father was moving down a slope towards a wounded corpsman. He then spotted an enemy machinegun position fifteen or twenty feet away. Unrelentlessly [sic] he continued his mission of grace by running to the corpsman and deliberately blocking him from the gunner's sight. Father proceeded to pray until, finally, he himself was shot and killed.

> Upon hearing the fatal news a young Marine tearfully came to me and asked, 'If life meant so much to Chaplain Capodanno, then why did he allow his own to be taken?'

> 'The answer is in your question', I replied. 'It was

---

[302] CAP/Staten, New York, September 13, 1967, Bishop William J. Moran to Father John J. McCormack, MM

[303] CAP/Staten, Washington, D.C., September 15, 1967, James W. Kelly to Force and District Chaplains.

precisely <u>because</u> he loved life—<u>the lives of others</u>—that he so freely gave of himself.'

Vincent Capodanno emptied himself; and his death has emptied us. Yet, paradoxically, we are filled—inspired—by his humility. His was an act of grace, an emulation of Jesus Christ.

His was the pilgrimage of a saint. Even to the end he faithfully held to the precept of our Lord that 'greater love hath no man than this, that a man lay down his life for his friends.'[304]

Following his death, many people wrote to the Capodanno Family remembering the Marine chaplain. Among them was Admiral Elmo R. Zuwalt, Jr. USN, who wrote,

In his months of service in Vietnam, Chaplain Vincent Capodanno earned the respect and affection of the sailors and Marines with whom he served. In an extremely perilous situation, he deliberately went into an area under heavy enemy attack to help the wounded, the dying, giving his own life in a heroic attempt to save others. His courage and his humanity are your heritage.[305]

Marine Corporal Ross B. Butera also remembered the priest:

Word spread that the chaplain [Father Capodanno] was always available and since he was as vulnerable to death as anyone else, he was always welcomed; not because he willingly shared the danger but because he shared the fear, the loneliness, the confusion, the comradeship and the mission. But he was different. Unarmed except for his strong faith, Father Capodanno was a contradiction of

---

[304] AMIL, Box: Funeral Binder. September 19, 1967, Funeral Mass Eulogy, Chaplain Eli Takesian.

[305] CAP/Staten, N.p., n.d., Admiral Elmo R. Zuwalt, Jr. USN, K of C Madonna Council #5915, Staten Island, Father Capodanno Memorial Committee, p. 5.

opposites [sic]. He was a man of peace but he chose to go to war. He appeared gaunt and ascetical but he was physically strong and capable of outwalking the youngest Marines. He was a man of few words but when he spoke he said all that had to be said. His deep-set sad brown eyes were distant but kind, almost as if he saw directly into your soul. The chaplain was a man of self-control and discipline, and yet he was a constant chain smoker. He was a Marine in the field, sloshing knee-deep in mud, eating canned rations, walking everywhere, carrying whatever he needed on his back and yet there was no doubt that he was a man of God. [306]

Father Thomas J. Wooten, a Navy chaplain in Vietnam, relayed the report by some wounded soldiers about Father Capodanno:

Vince really was a priest of God from what the dying, wounded and sick told me about him. One kid told me that Vince was to marry him and his fiancée in January in Texas. Time and time again, Vince showed the Marines of 3-5-1st Marine Division who Christ was and how He acted. We, as priests, are told to be Christ-like and if any priest ever enacted it with results it was Father Capodanno. The Church in the States will be richer for a priest like him.

There will be many people who will live a better and happier life in the future merely because they were fortunate to associate with a saintly Catholic Chaplain, Vince Capodano [sic]. I am a better priest because your brother and brother-in-law, folks, taught me what a real priest can do. [307]

---

[306] N.p., n.d., Corporal Ross B. Butera, USMC, K of C Madonna Council #5915, Staten Island, Father Capodanno Memorial Committee, p. 4.

[307] AMIL, Box: Medal of Honor Support. San Francisco, September 29, 1967, Father Thomas J. Whooten to Doctor and Mrs. Costa.

Father Louis R. O'Hare, MM, had been a seminarian with Father Capodanno, and was a chaplain in the United States Navy. He wrote the Navy Department that Father Capodanno

> . . . was a classmate and personal friend for six years during seminary training. I regard Chaplain Capodanno as one of the finest men I've known and I would be extremely grateful if you would grant me the opportunity of paying tribute to him by assigning me to the third battalion of the Fifth Marine Regiment which he left vacant.[308]

In his remarks at the dedication of a chapel in memory of Father Capodanno at the Newport, Rhode Island Chaplains' School, Father [Captain] David J. Casazza remembered the chaplain:

> To me, this Priest-Chaplain fitted my idea of Christ more than any other man I have ever met. He was strong, he was silent, he was a searcher. He was a quiet man with quick eyes. He spoke little but his presence was felt instantaneously. All of us usually fit into a mold of some sort. This man made his own mold. And every man who met him knew it. This man was different.
>
> He was a hungry man. –Hungry to be with his troops. –Hungry for more time, more time to seek out the lonely Marine, more time to sit with the scared boy, more time to explain things to the confused platoon leader.
>
> In answer to my question of what he did while out with the troops, he said,
>
> 'I am just there with them—I walk with them and sit with them; I eat with them and sleep in the [fox] hole with them—and I talk with them—but only when <u>they</u>

---

[308] AMIL, Box: Medal of Honor Support. New York, September 11, 1967, Father Louis R. O'Hare, MM, to Chaplain Division, Bureau of Naval Personnel, Navy Department, Washington, DC.

are ready to talk. It takes time, but I never rush them.' So, the time he longed for was their time, not his. Later, I couldn't help but think of how the apostles felt when Christ walked, sat, ate, slept and talked with them. [309]

Bishop William J. Moran, auxiliary bishop to Cardinal Spellman in the Military Ordinariate, wrote the Superior General of Maryknoll, Father John McCormack, MM, expressing his condolences,

Father Capodanno certainly gave his all for his men, and we consider him numbered not only among the great heroes of our country and an example of the truest type of military chaplain, but also a martyr of the Church. For what he did he did out of love of God and man. May his act of selflessness inspire us to do even a tenth of what he did.[310]

Miss June D. Arthur, who had corresponded with Father Capodanno, having received his form letters from Taiwan and Vietnam, wrote,

Father's letters were pearls in literature; his desire to serve and devotion to his calling are borne out by the fact that the man is dead.

If one could turn the coin over, and I presume that is all that can be done in viewing this situation, we can say that Father Copadanno [sic] was exactly where he wanted to be; doing the job he had selected as his life's work and he kept the commitment—'a good shepherd will lay down his life for his sheep.'

Father's last letter to me, received in early August,

---

[309] AMIL, Box: Funeral Binder. Newport, RI, February 5, 1968, Father David J. Casazza, CHC, USN, "Memorial Remarks at the Dedication of the Capodanno Chapel," p. 1.

[310] CAP/Staten, New York, September 13, 1967, Bishop William J. Moran to Father John J. McCormack, MM.

entreated that Space Blankets be purchased at sporting goods stores and be sent to the men in his [Marine] group. I wish there was some way in which a fund could be initiated so that the Space Blankets could be forwarded to pay tribute to Father Copadanno [sic]. They would, indeed, be Space Blankets—it would prove his love still envelops the men who served with him even though he is not physically there. [311]

The Honorable Paul R. Ignatius, Secretary of the Navy, recalled the Marine Chaplain in his remarks on the occasion of the posthumous bestowal of the Congressional Medal of Honor to Father Capodanno:

> A lieutenant in the Navy Chaplain Corps, he is the third chaplain in our country's history to receive the Medal of Honor, and the second Navy chaplain so honored.

> Indeed, men like Chaplain Capodano [sic] are unusual men. From the time he accepted his appointment in the Chaplain Corps in December 1965, until his death, he repeatedly distinguished himself. The Purple Heart and the Vietnamese Gallantry Cross with Silver Star, among other awards, attest to this.

> The act that Chaplain Capodanno so selflessly performed—the one that brings us here because it earned him his country's highest award—was consistent with the exemplary life he led.

> Learning that the Second Platoon of the M Company, 5th Marine Regiment, was engaged in savage fighting and might be overrun, he ran to join them. The unit was pinned down by enemy fire. Despite this, he proceeded to minister to the wounded and dying.

---

[311] CAP/Staten, Los Angeles, September 19, 1967, Miss June D. Arthur to "Director U.S. Naval Personnel."

His actions were an inspiration to the young Marines who saw him. His words of faith strengthened morale and provided encouragement to those who heard him.

Although seriously wounded in this action, he refused medical aid so that others could be treated, and continued ministering to his men. Seeing a wounded corpsman whose position was in the direct line of enemy fire, he dashed to his side. In so doing he made the ultimate sacrifice. [312]

A synopsis of events on the battlefield and of Father Capodanno's death were recalled by the Division Chaplain on September 5, 1967:

As the story of this chaplain's last hours of life gradually emerged to fill the outline of spare facts first reported by the division chaplain, it became apparent that Chaplain Vincent Capodanno's actions on that day had been inspired by an inordinate devotion to his men and to God.[313]

James Capodanno, Father Vincent's brother, wrote about his brother's attempts to save a fellow Marine threatened by machine gun fire on the battlefield on September 4th:

Father Vin ran to aid a Marine Corpsman in the line of fire—When the battle ended Chaplain Capodanno was found dead just inches away from the mortally wounded Corpsman. Father knew of the machine gunner—yet he valiantly strove to prevent the death of a fellow Marine, a

---

[312] CAP/Staten, Washington, DC, January 7, 1969, "Proposed Remarks by Honorable Paul R. Ignatius Secretary of the Navy at the Posthumous Medal of Honor Presentation to Lieutenant Vincent R. Capodanno, CHC, USNR," Washington Navy Yard," pp. 1-2.

[313] MARINE, File: Capodanno, Vincent, San Francisco, September 5, 1967, Division Chaplain to Force Chaplain, Fleet Marine Force, Pacific, p. 1.

fellow human. He gave his life in the attempt.[314]

Father Edward Killhackey, MM, a fellow Maryknoll priest who had known and worked with Father Capodanno, wrote James earlier:

> Few greater guys have braced [sic] this earth—There was a secret about Vin's style of life—I do know that his deep intence [sic] love of Christ pulsed in his veins. [315]

---

[314] CAP/Staten, Staten Island, N.d., n.p., James Capodanno to Robert E. Lee, p. 3.
[315] CAP/Staten, Chestnut Hill, MA, January 14, 1969, Fr. Edward Killackey, MM, to James Capodanno.

Epilogue

The United States was divided about the Vietnam War. Even today, the war is a source of debate. In the midst of the bloodshed and political rancor, the example of Father Capodanno stands out, for he was motivated neither by politics, nor by personal ambition, nor by military necessity. His was the dedication of Christ's priest to the Church and to others, whether as a Maryknoll missionary in the mountains of Taiwan, as a high school teacher in Hong Kong, or as a chaplain in the United States armed forces to men on the battlefield.

Father Capodanno grew in many ways in his imitation of Our Lord. One example is his habits of personal hygiene and dress, taught him by his mother and sisters. Judged to be fastidious because he was well shaven and neatly dressed in the seminary and in the missions, Father Capodanno became the object of ridicule and criticism among his fellow missionaries, and even by his superior, Bishop Donaghy, in Taiwan. He was taught to put aside his personal habits for others. His years working among the poor in the mountains and towns of Taiwan, and remaining faithful in the face of unfair treatment meted out to him by his Maryknoll superior in Taiwan, were preparations for his future work.

Those experiences anticipated Father Capodanno's greater dying to self to bring Christ to his Marines. In their fear, despair and loneliness in the military camps, and in the mud and filth of the battlefield front lines, Father Capodanno was there, even to the point of perfectly imitating Christ by his personal self-sacrifice to save a man in the heat of battle in Vietnam on September 4, 1967.

The tributes to Father Capodanno are numerous and varied. Among them:

- United States Congressional Medal of Honor for conspicuous gallantry, posthumously awarded.

- The Purple Heart Medal, posthumously awarded for his wounds sustained in battle.

- The Vietnamese Cross of Gallantry with Silver Star for meritorious service.

- The Navy Bronze Star for meritorious service.

- U.S.S. Capodanno: DE-1093 Escort Ship, commissioned in honor of Father Capodanno.

- A bronze statue of Father Capodanno's last moments on the battlefield, by Antonio Pierott, Army Chaplains School, Fort Wadsworth, Staten Island, NY.

- Marble statue of Father Capodanno in the Piazza Capodanno in Gaeta, Italy.

- Vincent Robert Capodanno Clinic, Gaeta, Italy.

- Capodanno Hall at the San Francisco Bay Naval Shipyard, California.

- Father Vincent Capodanno Research facility at the Navy Personnel Research Studies and Technology Department, Millington, TN.

- Father Capodanno Boulevard, Staten Island, NY.

- Father Vincent Capodanno monument, Staten Island, NY.

- Freedoms Foundation, Valley Forge, PA. [316]

Father Capodanno continues to inspire people, bringing many to Christ and the Church even decades after his death on the battlefield. An example is given in a 1974 book entitled, *Maryknoll—At Work in the World* by Ed Mack Miller:

> A stranger walked into chapel last night, prayed devoutly for a while, then left. We asked him who he was

---

[316] MARINE, File: Capodanno, Vincent. Washington, D.C., January 9, 1969, Medal of Honor Report.

and where he was from. He told us, then mentioned that he had been a teacher in the local high school during 1959-1960 and had known Father Capodanno who was here at that time. Then he went on to say that he had not been to church for several years, but after reading our article in the Catholic newspaper about Father Capodanno's death in Vietnam he decided it was time for him to get back to what the 'old' Church used to call his duties. . .

A missioner doesn't stop working even after he dies, does he? [317]

---

[317] Miller, Ed Mack, *Maryknoll—At Work in the World* (Maryknoll, NY., 1974), p. 47.

Appendix I

Mission Diaries, 1958-1959

Maioli Language School Diary for <u>September, 1958</u>
Father Donald J. Sheehan.[1]

September 7, 1958 is a date that will always remain indelibly etched in the memory of at least six Maryknollers. On that day an airliner landed at Taipei Airport, and from it stepped the six Maryknoll priests who had been assigned to Formosa. Behind us was a tranquil crossing of the Pacific Ocean, thanks to the STATES MARINE LINE, and its good ship, S.S. NATALIE. Due to a delay in obtaining air space to Formosa, an opportunity was afforded us to enjoy a ten day visit in Japan. Everyone took advantage of this opportunity to sightsee, visit mission stations, renew old friendships—even golf! Due to the kind hospitality of all the Maryknollers in Japan—especially Fr. Pheur in Kyoto, and Fr. Shepherd in Tokyo—we left Japan richer with many happy memories and a keener appreciation of the work that Maryknollers are doing there. However enjoyable our visit in Japan though, our sights were still trained beyond the horizon— to Formosa. It was with a feeling of anticipation that we bade farewell to Fr. Joe Shepherd and Fr. Jim Colligan at Tokyo Airport, and boarded a plane for the last leg of our journey. The flight to Formosa was smooth, and broken comfortably with a one and a half hour layover in Okinawa.

At the Taipei Airport we were welcomed to Formosa by Fr. George Haggerty, Fr. Al Fedders, and Brother Loyola. After clearing Customs, we were taken to the Maryknoll Procure in Taipei, where we offered Mass and enjoyed lunch. Shortly thereafter, the Miaoli contingent—Fr. Capodanno and Fr. Sheehan—bade farewell to the other men, and left with Fr.

---

[1] MFBA, Taiwan Diaries, Box 18, Folder 23: Taiwan-Taipei-Miaoli Language School 1954-1960.

169

Rhodes for Miaoli. Our arrival there was heralded with the traditional fire-cracker salute, and a get-together of the Maryknollers living within a reasonable distance.

The Maryknoll house here in Miaoli is situated next door to a pagan temple. Fr. Capodanno and I were both initiated into life in the Orient right from the beginning. With the 'luck of the Irish', our arrival coincided with a festival at the temple. And so it was seranaded [sic] into the early hours of the morning with the strident cacophony of Chinese music, and all the hoop-la that goes hand-in-hand with a Chinese festival. The pagan temple next door, incidentally, is owned by Maryknoll. Bishop Donaghy proudly claims to be the only Catholic Bishop in the world to own a pagan temple. Lest erstwhile Canon lawyers fall over each other rushing to the *Code* or to the *Fontes*, let it be said that the temple itself is to be moved—it is the property that the Bishop of Wuchow purchased for Maryknoll.

Neophyte missioners down through the years are all, I am sure, duly moved with initial impressions of the mission country where they are to labor. Frs. Capodanno and Sheehan are no exception to this, but would be embarrassed to mention what initially made the biggest impression on them—the humidity! Whether the humidity or the 'bed' situation made the biggest impression, is controversial. Having spent two years on promotion work in sunny Southern California, the writer mistakenly thought this would prepare him for the tropics. Let me hasten to correct that impression for anyone else so similarly misinformed. It is not true. No sooner than it took to place our bags down, than we were hastening to invest in two electric fans. Even with the mechanical aid furnished by such a convenience, you find yourself soaked with perspiration from just standing— or sitting or doing nothing.

The 'bed' situation, I am sure, needs explanation—and said explanation follows. For one used to reposing on a SIMONS [sic] BEAUTYREST or SEALEY [sic] POSTUREPEDIC, it was evident that some adjustment just had to be made to sleep on the hard matting stretched on a frame that was mistakenly (we thought) called a bed here. After a few nights spent on such a 'rack', we stumbled upon the 'adjustment' needed by comfort-loving Americans. It seems folks here use a thin pad on top of the matting, which removes the feeling that you are sleeping on a 'rack'. Old-timers, it seems, remove these mats for better ventilation in the summer time. When Brother Pascal presented the two new arrivals with mats for their beds, he was welcomed as joyfully, I am sure, as any wealthy widow who comes to the 39th Street house to leave a sizeable donation.

There are, of course, many other first impressions. Something that impressed me, I would label generically under the category of 'noise'. Noise is common all over the world, but I do believe that an Oriental town has more than its share. From long before dawn, till the wee hours of the morning, there is a constant din. There is the usual crow of the rooster, bark of the dog, toot of the horn, and cry of children. But add to these the sound of radios blaring out at top volume from small shops along the street, and the rumbling carts being pulled by water-buffalo on the road beyond the gate, or the rhythmical cadence of wooden clogs on hard pavement. All joined together this makes a very vivid first impression, albeit I must confess it has already become commonplace to me, and I now take it for granted.

Prior to our starting our study of the language, Fr. Capodanno and I had the opportunity to visit some of the missions here in the Miaoli territory. When you recall that just five years ago, when Fr. Hilbert and Fr. Glass first arrived in Miaoli, there were no Catholics and no buildings of any sort, you can not help but be impressed by the progress that has been made. In the town of Miaoli itself, Fr. Hilbert and Fr. Madigan have flourishing parishes, caring for over a thousand Catholics. With few exceptions, the larger towns and villages within the area of Miaoli are all cared for ably by Maryknollers.

Since our task is not to be a visitor of missions however, after a few days of orientation, we found ourselves settling down to the study of the language. Here in Miaoli, the Hakka dialect is the predominant language of the people. Though constantly buoyed up by assurances of how fortunate we are to be studying Hakka, and not Taiwanese, which is much more difficult than Hakka, we fail to see as yet the basis for this judgment. However, under the vigilant eye of Fr. Hilbert, one of the Maryknoll's pioneers among Hakka-speaking folks on the Mainland, and an accomplished linguist in that tongue, we're sure that in the course of time, if only by osmosis, enough of the language will filter through to equip us to join the ranks of the men actively working in the fertile mission fields of Miaoli.

Miaoli Language School Diary for <u>October, 1958</u>
Father Vincent R. Capodanno [2]

Oct. 1: summer came to official end: we turned clocks back to Standard Time. Both language students [Frs. Sheehan & Capodanno] expected extra sleep: gardener and housekeeper arrived at 6 and roosters crowed.

I left by afternoon bus to visit Fr. Dan Dolan at Towfen.

Oct. 7: Frs. Sheehan and Capodanno went to Fr. Lloyd Glass' "mountain parish" for the dedication and blessing of a shrine to the Blessed Virgin Mary. The statue in a kiosk is like that at Maryknoll. It is a bit smaller but no less attractive. The shrine and statue blessed, the parishioners held candles and formed a living rosary. We prayed silently in English as the group chanted Our Lady's prayer in Hakka.

Oct. 10: We followed news of the Holy Father's declining

---

[2] MFBA, Taiwan Diaries, Box 18, Folder 33: Taiwan-Taipei-Maioli Language School 1954-1960.

health and of his death on October 9th. We joined the rest of the world in praying for the repose of his soul. The Generalissimo ordered all public buildings to fly their flags at half-mast for three days beginning Sunday, October 12.

Later that same afternoon Bishop Donaghy returned from his visitation to Hong Kong. He was met at the front gate by his two barking dogs, who live here under Episcopal patronage, and by his two smiling language students.

We had supper with Fr. Don McGinnis and then attended October Devotions in his temporary church. The faces of many pagan children peered thru the open windows as they stared unintelligibly at the ceremonies. The bars on the windows seemed to accent their present exclusion from Mater Ecclesia.

Miaoli decked itself out in red, blue and white bunting, and Nationalist flags flew: Double Ten [October 10] on the calendar marks the birthday of the Republic of China.

Fr. Hilbert, director of the language school, gave us a free day: we went to Taichung. After a movie and supper Fathers Sheehan and Capodanno boarded the train and began the journey back to Miaoli. Two foreigners sitting in the dirty, hot, crowded local never fail to evoke whispered comments from the other passengers. Nor do the dirty, hot, crowded trains ever fail to evoke whispered comments from the two foreigners. This train ride looks like a scene one might expect to find in an Orson Welles movie production of a Graham Greene novel.

Oct. 12: Catholics throughout the Miaoli Deanery began preparing early in the day for the second annual public procession in honor of Our Lady of Fatima. All 13 parishes were represented . . . with ten of them marching behind colorfully decorated and illumined floats depicting Mysteries honoring Our Lady.

The language students were chaplains to Bishop Donaghy . . . and in their position at the end of the procession the three marched reciting their Rosaries silently, hoping that the one red and two white cassocks would not prove too much of a temptation to passing traffic.

The procession wound its way thru town and about three quarters of an hour later reached its destination at a large field decorated with an illumined cross at its entrance, multicolored lights strung along its borders and an altar set upon a stage at its far end.

The floats parked along the edges of the field and the Catholics filled the center. A sermon in Mandarin was followed by Benediction given by Bishop Donaghy. Light refreshments were given to the Catholics. Everyone talked about the procession, and Fr. Hilbert who organized it.

Oct. 13: 11 am: Bp. Donaghy celebrated Solemn Requiem for PP XII: Mass was sung by the sisters and clergy from Miaoli area.

Oct. 18: At 3:10 today, the entire enrollment of the language schools [Frs. Sheehan and Capodanno] takes the train to Taipei to take a second look at the capitol of Free China. The first look was a blur from a car window as we drove from the airport to the Taipei Procure and from there to Miaoli on the day of our arrival.

Sunday evening we leave the glitter of Taipei and return to our quiet country home next to the iron-works in Miaoli.

Oct. 20: Earlier in the month, the kitchen was moved along with the refrigerator to the new center house along with Brother Pascal. Now Fathers Sheehan and Capodanno live in a house with two noticeable empty spaces: Brother's room and the blank space in the kitchen. Bishop Donaghy promises a new refrigerator but Brother's helpfulness and company now require a short walk either for him or for us.

The small Japanese-style house is now occupied by the two language students with the Bishop living a few feet away in his two-room Episcopal palace.

Oct. 26: We accompanied Bishop Donaghy to the dedication of [the] new Jesuit church in Hsin Chu. The Archbishop of Taipei offered solemn Pontifical Mass. Dinner was served in a cleverly concealed dining room which we failed to locate; but the threat of a long procession in the afternoon proded [sic] us on till we found an American snack bar, where we stuffed ourselves on ham and cheese sandwiches with Lifesavers for dessert.

The Bishop, accompanied by experienced guides, had found the dining room after the Mass and later on found the language students sitting in his car, munching on Lifesavers. For some reason, from that moment on, the expression 'snack-bar', seems to have taken on a special power to produce reminiscences of surprise and humor, not to mention 'Lifesavers'. The afternoon was a procession followed by a low Pontifical Mass and a ride back to Miaoli.

Oct. 29: *Habemus Papam et habemus* a day off. At the bishop's invitation we drive with him to Taichung and visit with the Taiwanese language-students.

Oct. 31: Halloween brings unfulfilled expectations of visits from goblins, ghouls and ghosts. The former haunted police-station across the street from the Buddist [sic] cemetery and next to the Buddist [sic] shrine, presently the Maioli Center House, remains undisturbed except for the usual moaning of the man who lives in the shrine. He is in apparent good health but has gone there to moan and await the call of his ancestors. Fr. Rhodes, procurator, Fr. Wu, catechist director, and brother [sic] Pascal spend a quiet night undisturbed by spooks.

On the days unmentioned in this diary, we, the language students, waged the battle of Hakka, making small but significant advances toward the point of cracking the language barrier.

Miaoli Language School for November, 1958, Father Donald J. Sheehan [3]

November began with a slight earthquake tremor early in the day. Perhaps such was All the Saints' manner of compensating for the lack of firecrackers to herald their feast day. The rest of the month was quiet.

Until Nov 3rd: On this inauspicious day a grand experiment was held in the Center House. A frantic search was underway to find a good cook to prepare a Chinese banquet for special occasions. It was believed that such a cook had been found, but deemed advisable nonetheless to hold a 'trial run' prior to any definite commitments. And fortunate indeed we were that such was deemed advisable. Gastronomically speaking, the meal was a dismal failure. Though the Chinese have the reputation for being among the world's finest cooks, surely our noble experiment proved the adage that "Even Homer Nods."

The cook prepared the meal at his restaurant, about 1 mile away, and transported it to us on a bike, course by course. Between each course there was ample time for the Fathers to smoke two king-size cigarettes, or three regular size ones. The caliber of the meal can perhaps be best calculated by the fact that upon the completion of the meal, peanut butter sandwiches were heartily enjoyed by all. No doubt the most galling part of this culinary travesty was that it took two and one-half hours to discover that no substantial food was forthcoming. Lest this narrative puzzle "Old China-hands", and bring down the ire of Chinese-food lovers everywhere, I should hasten to explain that the chef was proven to be a real Chinese cook. However, the Fathers here hope that in the future, guests at our table for a

---

[3] MFBA, Taiwan Diaries, Box 18, Folder: 33, Taiwan-Taipei-Miaoli Language School, 1958-1959.

Chinese banquet will duly appreciate the heroic roles they played as guinea-pigs for the pleasure of their palate!

I am certain that all English-speaking people find themselves temporarily astonished upon hearing funereal dirges here on Taiwan. I presume most Oriental funerals, at least Chinese ones, are similar, no matter what the locale. Since the cemetery in Miaoli is up the road a short distance from our house, most of the funeral corteges pass by our gate. If the personage to be interred warrants much "face" and his survivors can afford it, a band is hired to accompany the procession. What is most disconcerting to a Western ear however, is the musical pieces that make up the band's repertoire. Popular hit-tunes seem to be the favorites. It will always seem strange to me that the song I WONDER WHO'S KISSING HER NOW would be found appropriate for such a sombre [sic] occasion. But that is what the band was playing one day when a funeral procession passed our house.

Brother Pascal mastered the Hakka dialect, and is now engaged in designing, planning and overseeing various building projects in the Miaoli area. He just completed renovations and an addition to the Maryknoll Sisters' convent in Miaoli. The beauty and speed of construction of the catechists' chapel adjacent to the Center House has led some to believe that another Brother Albert is in the making. Brother Pascal has gone to Fr. Rebol's parish in Yuan Li to direct construction of new church and rectory.

Nov 5th: Miaoli Maryknollers gathered at the Center House for the monthly gathering. Fr. Don McGinnis of Kungkwan gave the meditative reflections during holy hour.

Nov 9th: Many of the fathers went to Taichung for the dedication of [the] new pro-cathedral, which coincided with Silver Jubilee of ordination of Monsignor Kupfer. Many Taiwan hierarchy and countless religious and laity attended. It is surely a grand tribute to Monsignor Kupfer for the remarkable work that he and the Maryknollers in the Taichung Prefecture have accomplished within the space of a relatively short period of time. The day's festivities were concluded with a Chinese banquet on the grounds of the Catholic Center, attended by all the Religious.

Nov 10th: Archbishop Riberi and the Brazilian Ambassador to Taiwan had lunch with us. They stopped off at Miaoli for 2 hours on their road trip from Taichung to Taipei. As neophyte missioners, we were quite impressed with the evident high esteem that Archbishop Riberi held our late Bishop Ford. While Bishop Donaghy and the Archbishop were reminiscing about Bishop Ford, the Archbishop mentioned how keenly he felt Bishop Ford's loss, since he "was counting on him so much". One facet of Bishop Ford's character that seemed to impress the Archbishop very much was 'his great psychological insight'. To hear another Maryknoller praised so highly by a Churchman in a position such as Archbishop Riberi's, makes one extremely proud to be able to wear a Maryknoll Chi-Rho on his cincture.

During one evening chat with Bishop Donaghy, he gave the language students an interesting insight into life on mainland China, that had been passed on to him by Fr. McKernan in Hong Kong. A lady in Hong Kong, whose son was a Communist official in the Interior, had occasion to visit her son recently. Upon her return to Hong Kong, she mentioned to Father what things were like under the Communists. In this country section, the following was the day's work schedule in the fields—the pay, one catty of rice per day. They worked from 6 A.M. to 12 Noon. There was then a one hour rest period to eat their rice, but all had to do so there, except the mothers, who were allowed to return home for that hour. They then worked in the fields from 1 P.M. to 6 P.M., after which they could return home. But that was not the end of the day—they were required to return again at 10 P.M., and labor until 3 A.M. Sixteen hours of labor a day, seven days a week—and for one catty of rice a day. This speaks for itself, I am sure, and needs no comment.

Nov 22: We welcomed Fr. Witte to Taiwan, who spent 5

days visiting all the Maryknoll missions and speaking with the priests. Thanksgiving Day, the Maryknollers in this area gathered for a turkey dinner. On this occasion Bishop Donaghy took the opportunity to thank Father Witte for his very pleasant visit, and to assure him of all of our prayers upon undertaking his new duties as Council Member. Father Witte graciously thanked the Bishop, and expressed his pleasure at being able to meet all the Maryknollers, and bade us good-by as he was leaving after the meal to begin his visitation of the Maryknollers in the Taichung Prefecture.

Miaoli Language School Diary for December, 1958, Father Vincent R. Capodanno [4]

Dec. 3: December opened with strong breezes that blew all the Miaoli clergy in for the monthly meeting on the third. The discussion was about catechists and how to train them basically and develop them gradually.

Dec. 4: Bishop Donaghy leaves for the Bishops' Conference in Manila. Unconvinced that he could gain much face by bringing his own chaplains, he left without the language students.

Dec. 6: We took the grand tour of the local oil fields led by the company secretary who is a Catholic. We took the open cable car up to see the wells on the mountain side. Then a Chinese meal.

Dec. 8: The language school's silence remained unbroken by the sound of Hakka as we quietly celebrated Our Lady's

---

[4] MFBA, Ibid.

Immaculate Conception.

Dec. 17: Bishop Donagy returns from Manila, and in response to our questioning looks, tells us that we don't have to wear the Tonsure.

Dec. 18: Preparations being made for Christmas.

Fathers Sheehan and Capodanno spent their Christmas with Fr. Lloyd Glass. Fr. Sheehan helped Fr. Chu at the main church in Tahu while Frs. Glass and Capodanno left Christmas Eve morning for the mountain chapel built by and for the Aborigines.

One hour and many bumps after leaving Tahu, we arrived at Our Lady of Lourdes chapel. We were there at 9 A.M. but the Catholic Aborigines were already gathered together to greet us.

Our duties consisted of stringing up some lights to hooking them on to a portable generator; the decorations in and out of the chapel had already been arranged by the parishioners. Our work was accomplished in a short time and left us free to watch and participate in the festivities.

The setting was a small gully, actually the mountain road, in front of the chapel. The festivity was a series of races for men, women and children, and also the two Fathers. Everyone spent the morning racing, singing, laughing and in general having a good time.

After dinner and a few more hours of singing and talking, about two hundred people crowded into the small chapel for a game of Bingo. Since the Blessed Sacrament is not reserved in the chapel since there is no other building around, Fr. Glass draws a curtain across the sanctuary and permits the parishioners to use the rest of the chapel as a social room. The prizes lasted about an hour and then they began to clean up the chapel while the pastor heard confessions and the visiting assistant [Fr. Capodanno] slept.

The Aborigines are a colorful, friendly, intelligent people

who may not have much material wealth but who do have a spirit of independence. That trait showed itself by the fact that they kept their children home from school and that they arranged on their own all the activities of the day, including the prizes given out.

Just before I began Midnight Mass, the men lined the side aisles of the chapel with straw and in a few minutes the very young and the very old were stretched out fast asleep. The Manger next to the altar seemed very much at home.

After Mass, which they sang in excellent Latin, they sang some more while I said my second Mass. Later on, those who lived too far to walk home and return for the morning Masses, spread more straw on the floor and slept in the chapel.

Outside, a full moon lit up the sky and somewhere a mountain waterfall roared its alleluia for the Birthday of the King.

About 5 A.M. yours truly rolled over in his sleeping-bag while the Aborigines cleaned the chapel and sang Christmas carols around a bonfire made from the straw.

After Fr. Glass said his three Masses and I said my final Mass, everyone went home except a small group who busied themselves cleaning the chapel and the yard.

An hour's ride over the same bumps and we were back in Tahu where Frs. Chu and Sheehan celebrated their Christmas Masses for the townspeople and some of the near-by Aborigines.

One turkey dinner and a bus ride later, we were back in Miaoli where business and school went on as usual. One of the parishes put on a play at a local theatre that evening and if the pagans didn't know why, they at least knew that the Catholics gathered together to celebrate something.

The clergy of Miaoli Deanery gathered together on the 26th for a Christmas party, and after aweekend [sic] of visiting and being visited the doors of the language school swung open for class on Monday morning. Wednesday brings the first day of a four day holiday and the last day of 1958.

Even in a [sic] few short months we have been here the Church has noticeably grown in numbers and so on new Years Eve, 1958 we return thanks to God for His many graces here in Miaoli and pray for the continued expansion of His Kingdom, here and thru the world.

Maioli Language School Diary for January, 1959, Father Donald J. Sheehan [5]

A Language School is hardly a spawning ground for startling or noteworthy mission news. At this moment I feel somewhat like I felt at the beginning of the month of January. At that time I received a letter from a young vocation prospect in San Francisco. As a project of his 'Maryknoll Club', he wrote to a missioner. It fell to my lot to be that missioner. In his letter he requested an answer from me, explaining 'the work you are doing.' My first instinct was to relegate this letter to 'File 13' with dispatch. However, 'promotional' qualms of conscience smothered this instinct. But the same difficulty that confronted me in answering that letter, confronts me also in trying to write a diary for the month of January. As for our 'work' here, that should be apparent. As for news, well, as you shall swiftly see, there just wasn't much.

The Chinese pay little attention to change of old and new calendar years. The Chinese Lunar New Year is THE celebration, which will be February 8th this year.

---

[5] Ibid.

The month of January had hardly enough time to take off its wraps, before a few Maryknollers—at least this scribe!—cast envious eyes towards our Maryknoll brethren stationed in the warm climes of Africa or the Philippine Islands. It's cold here, but worse elsewhere.

Only 1 visitor graced our table during the month. Fr. Frederic Foley, SJ, from Taipei, who brought a copy of his newest privately published book, <u>The Face of Taiwan</u>. It is the pictorial fruit of Father's camera work over the years.

Jan 6: The Silver Jubilee of Religious Profession of Sr. Rita Marie, O.P., superior of Maryknoll Sisters working in Miaoli. Though Sister Rita desired a quiet celebration, all the Maryknoll Sisters on the Island journeyed to Miaoli to celebrate with the Jubilarian. Father Bernie Weiland added to the festivities by bringing himself, his movie projectors, and a Laurel & Hardy film to show the Sisters.

Jan 27: Regional Superior, Bishop Donaghy, celebrated his 30th anniversary of priesthood. A Solemn Pontifical Mass was offered in St. Anne's Church, attended by the local fathers and sisters, and representatives of the laity. Then Fr. Hilbert had a banquet for Bishop Donaghy and clergy in his parish hall. Fr. Dan Dolan gave a 5 minute dissertation on his 5 years of priesthood. He is good toastmaster.

As one can readily see, at this juncture, there is really nothing new in Miaoli. If the adage is true, that "no news is good news", and the rules of syllogistic reasoning still hold validity, then our superiors should find consolation in the fact that there is nothing but good news from Miaoli.

Miaoli Language School Diary for February, 1959
Father Vincent R. Capodanno [6]

The early days of February saw a round of activity that eventually erupted into the sound of smoke of many thousand firecrackers as the Chinese bid farewell to the Year of the Dog and greeted the Year of the Pig on February eighth, the first day of the new Lunar Year.

The Miaoli shops, of which there are more delicatessens than in the Bronx, did a landslide business since the New Year celebrations include two concepts that involve money spending or making, depending on the side of the counter that one faces. Everyone must wear at least one article of new clothing if not a completely new outfit, and it is also customary to exchange gifts. February 8th was halfway between Christmas and Easter but these externals fell into a pleasant blend of Santa Claus and an Easter parade.

On New Years Eve there is a traditional family reunion and dinner which may not be attended by anyother [sic] than parents, children and grandchildren. The meal lasts on 'till late evening when the younger generation is tucked into bed. The adults who feel so inclined may stay up all night and ring in the new year [sic] by talking, lighting fire crackers, eating, lighting firecrackers, singing, lighting firecrackers and in general making merry while lighting yet more firecrackers.

Fathers Sheehan and Capodanno compared notes and concluded that the last series of explosions during the night of February 7-8 was heard at 12:30 A.M. and the first at 4 A.M. The inbetweens [sic] were snuffed out by pillows and heavy sleep.

The first four days of the New Year were legal holidays.

---

[6] Ibid.

Many of the shops closed and the main street of Miaoli became the setting for friendly greetings, reunions, and walks.

The Hakka language school accommodated itself to these venerable Chinese customs by closing its portals for a week. The language students split trails at the train tracks with Fr. Sheehan going North to Taipei and Fr. Capodanno going South to Taichung. The trails reconverged [sic] at the Taichung Center House for the very fine retreat preached by Fr. J. Ryan Hughes, in from Japan to give the annual retreats. Father Hughes urged us to stir up the grace of our state and confidently work out our own salvation and courageously work for the salvation of those to whom we are sent.

The final night of the retreat saw the arrival of Cardinal Agagianian accompanied by Monsignor Kupfer and by Bishop Donaghy, who had recently returned to Taiwan from his visitation of the Hong Kong Maryknollers.

The Cardinal landed at Taipei, February 24, and was accorded full diplomatic honors, including an honor guard and a nineteen gun salute. All the hierarchy of Taiwan and many lay-Catholics were on hand to welcome the Cardinal who has come to visit the Catholics of Taiwan and to take a first hand look at the Church's work here.

A carefully plotted and precisely followed schedule led the Cardinal to the Maryknoll House on Thursday evening. He entered the gate, decorated with red lanterns, to the drive lined with Catholic boys dressed in cassocks and surplices, and amidst a colorful display of fireworks, walked to the front entrance where the Maryknollers stood beside the Papal and Chinese flags and greeted his Emminence. [sic] The Cardinal proceeded to the chapel where he received each priest individually and after a brief talk in English had dinner in the refectory with all the visiting clergy.

The following monrning [sic] he said a low Mass at the pro-cathedral where many Catholics bore witness to their Faith by crowding the church to overflowing. The large number of Communicants in turn bore witness to the Faith of the crowds.

After breakfast back at the Cneter [sic], the Cardinal and his party left Taichung to continue the visitation further south.

That same day the Miaoli Maryknollers returned home along with Fr. Hughes who is here to give a retreat to the Maryknoll Sisters in Miaoli.

The portals of the language school creaked open and the students of *Hakka I* surveyed their libraires [sic] covered with a coating of mildew matched in degree only by the covering of rust on their knowledge of the aforesaid *Hakka I.*

Miaoli Language School Diary for <u>April 1959</u>, Father Vincent R. Capodanno [7]

April 28th: 5:45 a.m.: An earthquake, which was the 30th anniversary of the quake that leveled Miaoli and other places in Taiwan. Not severe enough but lasted long enough to knock things off shelves and crack walls.

In between Hakka exercises we read the just-arrived assignment sheet from Maryknoll. Bishop Donaghy has announced that Mandarin-speaking Fr. Ted McCabe will join us in Miaoli. Five of the other men will go to Taichung and one to Hong Kong.

April 29th: Began the *Mat su* celebrations: the most popular goddess in Taiwan.

The cult originated in the Fukien and Dwangtung

---

[7] Ibid.

provinces of China and was brought to Taiwan by immigrants from those places many years ago.

Stories of her birth center on the sea, so most devotees are fishermen.

There are some aspects about the celebration that set Catholics wondering if it could possibly be Catholic in its origin, but there are no convincing arguments or authentic indications to prove this point. However, the processions, the statues, the miracles and finally, her title of "Queen of Heaven", all have a very familiar ring to Catholic ears.

There are two opinions which I've heard and though they are only possibilities they are interesting enough to repeat.

One would suggest that *Mat su* was a Catholic girl strongly devoted to the real Queen of Heaven. Through *Mat su*'s prayers to Mary, certain miraculous events took place. Since she lived among pagans ignorant of the true source of the powerful intercession, they attributed the miracles to *Mat'su*'s prayers and intercession with the supreme god of the pagan heaven. Over a period of years the present cult was developed.

The other opinion is that the pagans saw statues of Our Lady on the Portuguese ships coming to the Orient in the 1500s. Reasonably assuming that such long voyages could be made only under the patronage of an extremely kind and powerful intercessor, an incomplete devotion to Mary was incorporated into the pagan religious life of fishermen and gradually grew in popularity while it was being warped into its present shape.

Both are opinions and just opinions unstrengthened [sic] by written or oral testimony. Neither offers [sic] a reasonable explanation of the generally accepted fact that this week is the thousandth anniversary of the birth of *Mat su*. However, not all pagans agree that the devotion is 1000 years old.

For those unable to visit the shrine or for those who want to show special gratitude to *Mat su*, each community arranges to have a copy of her statue brought from a shrine in their own town or city. Yesterday and today were Miaoli's opportunity [sic] to have the statue. Preparations began yesterday with a parade on the main street which earlier had been lined with tables laden with food and incense offerings. Today's parade passed in front of the language school. For twenty minutes there was a steady stream of people passing by.

The air was heavy with the dull booms of drums, loud explosions of firecrackers, piercing clangs of cymbals and shrill blasts of flutes but even more noticeable was the presence of something negative. There was no joy. There was confusion, noise, incense, but no real joy; just a long line of people beating out their devotion to a non-existent deity.

Mat su has come and gone and Miaoli will settle itself down to its ordinary daily life.

April ends with the return of Brother Pascal from Yuan Li, where he supervised the building of the new church in theparish [sic] of Fathers Rebol and Bell.

Miaoli Language School Diary for May, 1959,
Father Donald J. Sheehan [8]

May 1: Brother Pascal returned to Miaoli after his time in Yuanli. He spent the past months in Fr. Rebol's parish in Yuanli, overseeing construction of new parish plant in this southernmost parish of the deanery.

The warm, May sunshine, besides causing flowers of the fairest to bloom, seems to have worked magic in other ways.

---

[8] Ibid.

Two of the "younger men" of the deanery were sprinkled with the gold dust of vim and vigor to "flower" onto Fr. Maynard Murphy's new tennis court at Tunglo. The results of the match were not divulged, but it is rumored that only the insurmountable difficulty of bilocation keeps Bishop Donaghy and Father Madigan from the Center Court at Forest Hills!

May 4: Fr. Donat Chatigny hosted Miaoli Fathers and Sisters at his parish in Nanchuang. It was Father's 55th birthday and the day Bishop Donaghy blessed his new church. Fr. Donat was ill later in the month, and the doctor said he had a heart attack. The Sister doctor looked at him and said he hadn't had one, but needed rest.

The middle of May found the Island of Formosa become *formosior*. What caused this increase of pulchritude? Well, on May 12th, Fr. Ed Baskerville, *en route* to the United States on furlough, stopped by for a week's visit to the island. Father Ed brought us all up to date on the Maryknollers' activities across the world in British East Africa. In his short stay, Father Baskerville brought his smiling countenance and jovial conviviality to almost all the Maryknoll missions on the island. Though "knowledge aforethought" was disclaimed, Father Ed was in time to attend a "steak-fry" for the Taichung language school students which Fr. Lloyd Glass hosted at his mission at Tahu. I don't know if Duncan Hines includes Tahu among his recommended dining spots, but you could look long and look far before you would surpass Chef Glass' hand at the charcoal-broiler.

May 18: Many Fathers gathered at Fr. Rebol's parish in Yuanli for a clergy open house. The official dedication is not 'till June 7th, but Frs. Rebol and Bell allowed the Fathers a sneak preview. A tasty buffet luncheon was provided for those who attended.

May 25: Rome gave approval for Maryknoll Sisters to start [a] new Congregation at Maioli: Sisters of the Sacred Hearts of Jesus and Mary. They hope to have their first postulancy under way this fall.

The feast of Corpus Christi found one of the language students, Fr. Capodano [sic], preaching a Chinese sermon at the Tunglo parish, while the other student was busy with camera at Fr. Don McGinnis' mission, filming the crowning of the Blessed Virgin's statue and the Corpus Christi procession.

The end of May finds the two language students hanging bravely on for the last month of language school. The feeling is something similar to the grit and determination that one musters up in the dentist's chair, as the dentist gives the last, whirring bore with his drill (so close to the nerve!) prior to filling a cavity in a tooth. You know its necessary, but you're so happy to see him push the drill away. We look for the drill being pushed away on June 29th, Foundation Day.

Miaoli Language School Diary for June, 1959,
Father Vincent R. Capodanno [9]

June 3: The day of our monthly meeting and the day language students received their assignments. Fr. Sheehan goes to Fr. Lloyd Glass at Tahu; Fr. Capodanno to Fr. Maynard Murphy in Tunglo.

June brought rain and visitors. Among them, Fr. Pete Reilly on his way back to Hong Kong and Fr. Mike Hiegel from the Philippines. Fr. Hiegel is making a tour of the Maryknoll language schools in the Far East in his capacity as director of the Maryknoll language school in Davao.

Our Hakka language course officially ended Saturday, June 27th. Fr. Hilbert now relinquishes the helm he has held for

---

[9] Ibid.

these past nine months to the two new graduates and the teachers they will have in their new parishes. Our thanks to Fr. Hilbert lies in the fact that we have already both preached twice and feel confident to go to many more sermons.

Monday, June 29th: All Maryknollers in Taichung and Miaoli areas gather together at Taichung Center House to celebrate Foundation Day.

This is a double celebration in Taiwan: Foundation Day and the celebration that 5 of our men are Silver Jubilarians: Frs. Haggerty, O'Neill, Keelan, Daley and Chatigny.

The Jubilarians sang High Mass with Fr. O'Neill as celebrant, Fr. Haggerty as deacon, Fr. Daley as subdeacon. Bishop Donaghy preached briefly, congratulating them, and reflected on God's blessings upon the Societyand [sic] urged each to recall to mind the missionary ideal as exemplified in the lives and deaths of Saints Peter and Paul.

This gave us the opportunity to welcome Fr. Chatigny back from the hospital where he recently underwent surgery and a general check up. We also wished Fr. Al Fedders good luck as he leaves for his new post as rector of Maryknoll.

June 30: We bade farewell to the glass-topped walls of the Miaoli language school, the scene of the first phase of the language battle but also the scene of a pleasant year with Bishop Donaghy, Fr. Rhodes, Fr. Wu and Brother Pascal. Lest the Bishop find the house too quiet while he is here alone, we leave him with one parakeet, fifteen goldfish, one cat, two dogs and six new puppies.

Tunglo Mission Diary, <u>September and October 1959</u>, Father Vincent R. Capodanno [10]

September: recovering from the August floods. USA relief distributed by Fr. Murphy.

2 Local police tried to implicate Fr. Murphy with false accusation of possessing communist literature. It was a frame up.

Charge was eventually seen as false, dropped, and the 2 policemen arrested.

Between these two events, we went about opening a Catholic library in town. Through it we hope to disperse Catholic literature to those who have no inclination to come to the parish itself.

We rented a little shop, fixed it up, furniture was purchased, and we had [an] opening banquet on October 14th. Sunday, Oct 18th, the pastor blessed and opened the Catholic library of Tunglo, Taiwan.

We haven't developed a full program of activities yet but that will come as time passes. One definite activity will be English classes, the perennial favorite.

A number of people come in to thumb through magazines and borrow books. Several have asked questions of the ever-present Catechist. These questions may be the beginning of the road to Baptism, if not, a knowledge of the Church is nevertheless being spread.

The Tunglo parish is ready for a series of Bingo parties and bequests to mark the pastor's departure for his furlough to USA.

---

[10] MFBA, Capodanno Personnel File, Box 12, Folder 2: Tunglo Diary, 1959.

Oct 30th: Bingo party for the parishioners.

Oct 31st: President C.K. Check's birthday and the day to honor seniors. We had a banquet for the old of the parish and asked each to bring a friend. We also invited the very young of the parish, those fifteen and under. The affair was a success and ended happily as the guest of honor, Bishop Donaghy, passed out gifts of heavy woolen undershirts to each of the older guests.

That night, another Bingo was held for children only. They played long enough so that almost all received a prize.

Sunday: Fr. Murphy baptized 3 women who have been studying faithfully for some time now. After the Catechist and the Pastor explained to them that as Catholics they couldn't consult temple magicians nor buy medicine from them, they themselves told their families that in the future their own medical consultations would be with medical doctors and that if anyone in the family wants to go to the temple they go alone.

Nov 2nd: A busy day: About 140 people, Catholics and pagans, paid part of the expense of a banquet for the pastor and were in turn invited to attend an evening Mass for All Souls.

Before Mass, Fr. Murphy explained the significance of the Feast of All Souls and the ceremonies of the Mass for the benefit of the pagans. During the Mass the Catholics chanted their prayers and the pagans followed in prayer books. After the Mass, everyone went out to the cement tennis court to feast on the Chinese banquet.

Before the banquet, the local mayor gave a talk praising Fr. Murphy. The Pastor responded telling them he was leaving right after the banquet, to their surprise.

After dinner, about seventy-five people waited out front for the cab which would bring their Pastor to Miaoli—the first stage of his trip home.

At 9 p.m., the cab came, and amid the honest tears of many and the sound of firecrackers, Fr. Murphy left Tunglo for a while.

I am going to add a P.S. to this diary in the form of a personal reflection. As Maryknoll grows in numbers and mission territories it becomes more difficult to follow the activities of all its members. Some men will stand out in the future as others have in the past. They are well known, or will be, and justly receive acclaim for what we might term famous work. In contrast to them, there will be in the future as there is now another group who have done their work faithfully and well but who are practically unknown. Their work has never made the headlines, but without their work Maryknoll would not achieve its purpose. Yet, if their names are mentioned outside their own region they are either vaguely recognized or totally unknown. Their number will increase with time; their fame, never.

Those were the thoughts of a neophyte missioner as he bid bon voyage to a very fine pastor who was returning home for a brief time; for the fourth brief time in thirty-two consecutive years.

Tunglo Mission Diary for <u>November, 1959,</u>
Father Vincent R. Capodanno [11]

Early in this month one of the Catechists announced that one of our Catholic girls was on her way over to sign the *Cautiones* with her pagan husband-to-be. A simple enough affair particularly since arrangements had been made with Fr. Murphy before he left on furlough. However, this particular girl is totally deaf and completely unable to speak. I could handle the boy, but I told our married man-Catechist, her cousin, he would have to

---

[11] MFBA, Ibid.

explain the *Cautiones* to the girl in the presence of the priest and have her show some sign of consent to their obligations. I considered doing sort of a lullabye [sic] routine when he finished just to make sure she understood. However, after the Catechists [sic] graphic and self-evident charade, I felt any rock-a-bye baby antics on my part would have been superfluous, not to mention naïve. It all ended happily with both aware of what they willingly agreed to and the boy blushing as he stared down at his brand new sneakers.

Fr. Dan Dolan arrived the night of Nov 6th to take over as temporary pastor while Fr. Murphy is in the States.

The new Catholic library is well received by townsfolk and is daily well used. The Catechist reports the following statistics, all in round numbers:

1. 130 people enter the library daily. Of which 40 are high school children and 90 adults. Among the 90 adults, 10 daily are making their first visit.

2. Most read secular papers, then magazines, then, if they have time and nothing else to read, Catholic pamphlets.

3. Books of various subjects are here, but novels are much more in demand than Doctrine books.

4. Posters in the shop get more attention by new-comers than by the steady customers.

5. Since we opened 1 month ago, 13 questions have been asked. The questions and answers were heard by all present since the shop is small. Most often asked was the difference between the Catholic and Protestant religions. We have two Protestant groups in Tunglo so the question is a natural one. Some wanted to know the difference between the Buddist [sic] priests and the Catholic priests and finally a few asked why priests don't marry.

We are running 2 series of posters in the library: one on

the Mass and the other on Christmas. For the Mass, we've used a series of pictures that appeared last year on Parish Sunday bulletins in USA. The Christmas series began on the First Sunday of Advent: It started with Creation and will end the Nativity Scene. Since we are changing the poster each day the question of appropriate pictures would have been a great one. The complete set will cover all the main Old Testament themes necessary for an understanding of Christmas, if such a thing be possible in one month's time. A caption in Chinese characters helps fill in the gaps.

Among the steadies at the library is a group of young men in the Taiwan awkward age. They have finished school, are not working and expecting to go in the army in the near future.

They comprise the Catholic Church English classes presented twice a week at the library. This was their first personal contact with the Church, and to create a stronger tie, they were invited to form themselves into a volley-ball team to represent the Tunglo Mission at games with other Catholic missions.

Fr. Bell of the Yuan Li Mission and Tunglo agreed to convey self-initiated challenges to boys from both parishes. A trumped-up challenge seemed to be a good way to get the Tunglo Tigers organized. The first game comes in mid-December to be followed by another with Fr. Sheehan's team from Taifu.

On Nov. 28th we blessed [the] Advent wreath and asked [the] oldest Catholic man in the parish to light first candle. The old boy enjoyed it so much that the excitement carried him away. . . . that is, he went home right after lighting the candle without staying for Mass. He is usually here for Sunday Mass so we presume he rushed home to tell everyone about it all.

November ends on a melodious note as Fr. Dolan nightly directs the parish rehearsal of Christmas carols.

Tunglo Mission Diary for <u>December, 1959,</u>
Father Vincent R. Capodanno [12]

[Hand written "OMIT" for following paragraph]: A bright sunny December 12th afternoon saw the opening volley-ball game at the Tunglo Mission court. Fr. Dick Bell's team accepted the challenge and arrived in the early P.M. to play against the Mission team and also the grammar school teachers' team. Fr. Bell's C.Y.O. team lost all games to the all-pagan Tunglo teams. Grace builds on nature.

After the tournament, we began preparations for Christmas. A flurry of electrical wire, crepe paper, trees, wreaths, pine sprays, tree decorations, window decorations, cans of silver and gold paint, gifts, Santa Claus suits, candy, cookies, holy cards and Mangers all settled on December 24th to reveal a nicely decorated chapel and doctrine hall. Even the stained glass window of Our Lady was illumined from outside, thanks to Fr. Dolan's skill and his wire, too.

A theater-poster artist in Miaoli followed instructions and old Christmas cards and on Dec. 22 a beautifully painted Nativity scene measuring 8 by 12 feet was planted firmly in place in front of the local Post-office. An explanation of the meaning of Christmas and an invitation to attend Mass ran along two sides of the picture.

Our main gate was decorated with green leaves and red-paper Chinese characters proclaiming the Birth of Christ. A Catechist and four other men, two of whom were pagans, did the work.

A section of the flat roof of the church was decorated with a large Manger. The light from the electric cross reminded

---

[12] Ibid.

everyone day and night, that this was a special season.

Our library was the central distributing point for Christmas literature to anyone who sought it. Books on Christmas were available for reading or borrowing and two pamphlets plus one-sheet throwaways were there for the taking.

A few weeks before Christmas one of the Catechists had gone around to the various shops and arranged with over one hundred to display a large attractive poster put out by the Jesuit Press.

The gates of the church were not broken down by crowds of pagans trying to come in for Christmas Mass, but everyone in Tunglo knew it was Christmas, and more important, knew also the meaning of the Birth of Christ.

Christmas Eve blew cold and windy all day. The mission was crowded for the pre-Mass slide show put on by Fr. Dolan but long about 11 P.M. many of the pagans went home. The prospect of warm beds seemed more in keeping with the weather than did Mid-night Mass, and so off they went but not without the impression that this was an important festival for the Catholic Church.

For the many, both Catholic and pagan, who did stay for Mass, a post-Mass snack of tea, cookies and candy seemed to be an appreciated reward.

Christmas morning, a few of the faithful—few showed up for 9 A.M. Mass, but the chapel was crowded to capacity for Bishop Donaghy's evening Mass on Christmas.

1959 closes with a cold dark day, which in no way symbolizes the bright hopes for the growth of the Chruch [sic] in Tunglo, one of the many Nazareths of Taiwan.

Appendix II

Some Reflections on Adaptation to the Orient, Father Vincent R. Capodanno, MM, November 1966 [1]

In our attempt to create a good image and to establish rapport with the people of Viet Nam, there are certain things we should try to remember and certain things we should attempt to do. It is most necessary for us to remember the influences that have gone into our own formation and equally necessary for us to make an intelligent effort to understand the people in whose homeland we are living. Both approaches combined can result in a behavior pattern that is comprehensible to us and acceptable to the Viet Namese.

In this vein, there are several observations I can make as a result of personal experience acquired while doing missionary work in the Orient.

We are oftentimes confronted with the formidable statement that Oriental culture is five thousand years old. The impact of this knowledge causes us to be either sarcastic in our judgement [sic] or condescending in our attitude. In reality the Orient as we see it today is the result of a long period of religio-philosophical and historical influences which, while differing from our own, have had the cumulative effect of creating a society steeped in its own traditions and customs. Frequently the lack of appreciation and understanding of the Orient is due to a similar lack of appreciation and understanding of our own traditions and customs and their long history of development.

Occidental man must then ask himself: "What has gone into my own formation?" The answer is that he, too, is the product of an ancient civilization which, in terms of recorded

[1] AMIL, Capodanno Correspondence Binder, "Some Reflections on Adaptation to the Orient".

history goes back almost four thousand years to the time of the Biblical personage of Abraham and which was given a universally acknowledged impetus by the teachings of Christ.

Our Occidental world is formed and informed by this Judaeo-Christian influence. From infancy many are trained in its principles but all are affected by its concepts. Even in those areas of the Occident where Christianity may be numerically extinct or where its force may be dormant the Judaeo-Christian phenomenon continues in existence exercising influence and creating attitudes by what may be called its residual sovereignty over the mind of Occidental man. In those places where Christianity is vital and vibrant, the Judaeo-Christian effect on personal development is incalculable

A man then, consciously or unconsciously, formed by Judaeo-Christian principles and concepts, in coming to the Orient comes to an area where the forces of his own formation have had only limited influence. The initial impact often causes either indignation or astonishment or both. In contemporary terminology it is said he enters into a state of cultural shock.

This condition can be remedied to the satisfaction of all concerned by adaptation and acclimatization. There are many areas in which these can take place but briefly there are three general areas wherein adjustment to the Orient can be effected more smoothly and gracefully. They are: respect for persons; respect for authority; respect for things.

Respect for persons

As members of an established ethical system highly individualized and enhanced by a number of American traditions, many Americans have a tendency to expect others to conform to our own standards and procedures. In short time it becomes evident that adults are not going to do this either at all or at the pace desired and consequently many will turn to the most malleable of all, the children. There is then lavished upon children a degree of attention and a wealth of material gifts that is often offensive to established custom.

The attitude should be one of approachability extended to all but particularly to the adults. It is the elder group which should receive the initial and the most attention; of these elders it is the men who are to receive the first attention; and of these elder men, it is the oldest who should be given deference. The oldest man is not necessarily the leader but the leader himself will take no offense at someone showing respect for the aged. However, he may be offended at being passed over for the benefit of a child.

In establishing relationships with persons of a different background our gregariousness should be tempered with reserve and formality which creates a broad foundation for further development.

Respect for authority

It is the officer in charge who should set the tone for all contacts with local persons. As the unit leader it is he who is expected to hold initial and introductory talks with his counterpart of a particular area. There should be no distribution of goods or services until the local leader has come to and consulted with the officer in charge. The officer then can enlist the aid of the leader so that whatever is to be done can be accomplished in as orderly a fashion as possible with as little loss of temper and face as possible.

By showing respect for established authority and requiring respect for one's own authority one can hopefully anticipate a greater degree of cooperation.

Respect for things

Many material things which we have and take for granted are nothing less than miraculous to the inhabitants of small Oriental villages. When the materially poor see carelessness in the use and distribution of things and money the natural conclusion is that the materially richer are behaving foolishly. A further conclusion is that the foolish merit neither respect nor consistent cooperation.

In exhibiting respect for things we establish contact with values admired and understood throughout the Orient.

We, as Americans, have chosen an end: to help the Viet Namese people to help themselves. Having chosen an end, we must choose the most proper and effective means of achieving that end. The observations presented here are obviously not comprehensive of the situation and not entire in their own development. What is offered here consists of several personally arrived at possibly effective means of achieving our end. Others may disagree with the areas chosen or the conclusions reached and these others may be correct in their judgement [sic] and evaluation.

Our adaptation to the Orient is a field that for all of us is vast and for many of us un-chartered. The paths each man discovers and the experience he acquires can be shared with all not as definitive solutions but more as steps in the learning process.

There is necessary [sic] a great amount of study if one is to attempt to understand the Orient in all its complexity. The research work so ably begun by Chaplain Mole and so ably continued by Chaplain McGonigal under the title of the PERSONAL RESPONSE PROJECT[2] is an admirable and original contribution toward our appreciation of the Orient in general and Viet Nam in particular.

---

[2] The "Personal Response Project," begun in 1965 by Chaplain Robert L. Mole and continued by Chaplain Richard McGonigal, was a research project designed to "understand the Vietnamese culture by learning about its people, why they believe and act as they do, their religious principles and ethical systems," in order to "increase in some degree trust and confidence between American military personnel and indigenous citizens." Chaplains began conducting Personal Response training to troops in late 1966.

An ancient maxim, attributed by some to Confucius, says: "It is better to light one candle than to curse the darkness." Chaplain McGonigal's PERSONAL RESPONSE PROJECT provides the necessary light to avoid unnecessary collisions.

Biographical Timeline
of Father Vincent R. Capodanno, MM
1929-1967

February 13, 1929:	Birth, 105 Winant Street, Staten Island, NY.
April 28, 1929:	Baptism, Church of Saint Michael, Mariners Harbor, Staten Island, NY.
April 21, 1937:	First Holy Communion and Confirmation, Church of Saint Clement, Staten Island, NY.
February 13, 1939:	Death of his father, Vincent Capodanno, Sr.
January, 1943:	Graduated P.S. 44 grammar school.
February 4, 1947:	Graduated Curtis High School.
1947-1949:	Employed at Pearl Insurance Company, New York, NY.
1948-1949:	Night classes at Fordham University, New York, NY.
March, 1949:	Application to Maryknoll for seminary acceptance.
May, 1949:	Maryknoll acceptance for his entrance to college seminary.
June 25-August 3, 1949:	Summer Latin course at Maryknoll preparatory high school seminary, The Venard, Clarks Summit, PA.
September, 1949:	Maryknoll College seminary, Glen Ellyn, IL.
June, 1953:	Completed undergraduate studies in philosophy and graduated.

June-August, 1953:	Worked at the Pearl Insurance Company, New York City, during the summer to pay for college tuition and financially help his mother.
September, 1953:	Maryknoll novitiate, Bedford, MA.
August 30, 1954:	Completed novitiate; took his first solemn oath for Maryknoll.
September, 1954:	Major seminary studies began at Maryknoll's "The Knoll," Ossining, NY.
September 17, 1954:	Tonsure.
May, 1955:	Promoted to second year of theological studies, and approved for promotion to First Minor Orders and the second temporary oath.
June 9, 1955:	Received First Minor Orders: Porter and Lector.
September 15, 1955:	Second temporary oath.
June 7, 1956:	Received Second Minor Orders: Exorcist and Acolyte.
September 13, 1956:	Third and final temporary oath.
June 6, 1957:	Subdiaconate ordination and Perpetual Oath for Maryknoll.
September 14, 1957:	Diaconate ordination.
October 1, 1957:	Granted temporary leave of absence and a financial loan from Maryknoll to attend to his injured mother.
March 31, 1958:	Maryknoll General Council granted approval for ordination to the priesthood, and an assignment to the Formosa Region. Language school in Miaoli.

June 7, 1958:   Awarded a Bachelor of Arts degree
                         in Sacred Theology and a Master's
                         degree in Moral Theology.

June 14, 1958:   Priesthood ordination.

June 15, 1958:   First Low Mass with his family at
                         "The Knoll"; granted faculties during
                         the formal Maryknoll Departure
                         Ceremony of new missioners.

June 22, 1958:   First High Mass, offered at
                         Our Lady of Good Counsel Church,
                         Staten Island, NY.

September 7, 1958:   Arrival in Taipei Airport, Taiwan.
                         Began language studies in Miaoli
                         and limited mission parish work.

June 28, 1959:   Assignment as curate at St. Mary's
                         Parish, Tunglo.

June 29, 1959:   Completion of language school
                         studies.

August, 1959:   Vacation and pastoral work in
                         Hong Kong.

September, 1959:   Arrival in Tunglo.

September, 1960:   Transferred to Miaoli as House
                         Superior of the Miaoli Maryknoll
                         Center House and Director of the
                         Boys' Student Hostel.

February 27, 1961:   Death of Rachel Capodanno, Father
                         Capodanno's mother.

June 16, 1961:   Transferred to Holy Rosary Parish,
                         North Miaoli as curate.

May, 1962:   Temporarily administered Holy
                         Rosary Parish, and transferred to
                         St. Mary's Parish, Tunglo as curate.

May, 1963:	Transferred as pastor of Saint John the Baptist Parish, on the outskirts of Miaoli.
August 17, 1964:	Traditional six-month furlough after six years in the missions. Returned to his sister's home in Kearny, NJ.
March 8, 1965:	Arrived in Taiwan. Instructed to report to Bishop Donaghy. Transferred to teach English at Maryknoll's high school in Hong Kong and assigned to learn Cantonese.
March 21, 1965:	Arrived in Hong Kong to begin his new teaching duties and language school studies in Cantonese.
April 1, 1965:	Father Capodanno requests transfer to Taichung.
April 6, 1965:	Bishop Donaghy refuses request for transfer to Taichung.
April 26, 1965:	Medical report by Doctor John Carey-Hughes: Father Capodanno's health was negatively affected by his transfer to Hong Kong.
June 3, 1965:	Father Capodanno writes the Maryknoll Superior General requesting an assignment to another Maryknoll region.
June 8, 1965:	Father General writes Father Capodanno that he will bring his request for a transfer to the Maryknoll General Council.

June 27, 1965:	Father McLoughlin, Hong Kong superior, met with Father Capodanno.
July 13, 1965:	Naval physical examination of Father Capodanno.
July 14, 1965:	Father Capodanno wrote Bishop John Comber, Superior General of Maryknoll, requesting permission to become a United States Navy chaplain.
July 14, 1965:	Father Capodanno wrote to the chief of Chaplains at the Pentagon in Washington, D.C. asking for information about requirements for military chaplaincies.
July 30, 1965:	Letter from the United States Navy instructing him to proceed with application for military service.
August 2, 1965:	Telegram from the Chief of Chaplains to Father Capodanno informing him that any application to the United States Military must be made within United States territory and that prior ecclesiastical endorsement from his Maryknoll superior general must be obtained.
August 9, 1965:	Father Capodanno wrote the Maryknoll Superior General explaining his actions during the summer: physical examinations and inquiries concerning military chaplaincies, and asks the Father General to grant him permission to join the United States Navy.

August 13, 1965:	Bishop Comber's written permission that Father Capodanno may apply for a chaplaincy in the United States Navy and to apply to the Military Ordinariate for admittance as a military chaplain. To facilitate the process, and to reaffirm the young priest's bonds with Maryknoll, Father Capodanno was assigned to the Maryknoll mission in Kumueal, Hawaii to work in a parish while applying to the military.
August 18, 1965:	Father Capodanno acknowledged the Father General's letter thanking him for his permission, and he formally requested to be assigned to Vietnam.
August 22, 1965:	Father Capodanno arrived in Hawaii.
September 4, 1965:	Bishop Comber's written notification to the Military Ordinariate of his permission for Father Capodanno to apply for a Navy chaplaincy.
September 14, 1965:	Written permission from the Military Ordinariate to Father Capodanno to apply for a chaplaincy in the Naval Reserve.
September 23, 1965:	Written endorsement granted by the Military Ordinariate.
November 22, 1965:	Written acceptance of Father Capodanno's application by the Chief of Chaplains. Assigned to the Chaplain School at the Naval Schools Command, Newport, Rhode Island.

November 29, 1965:   Military Ordinariate granted Father Capodanno personal parochial jurisdiction and faculties while at the Naval School.

December 9, 1965:   Father Capodanno wrote the Chief of Chaplains accepting the assignment.

January 3, 1966:   Arrival at the Chaplain School in Newport, Rhode Island.

March 10, 1966:   Assigned to Camp Pendleton, California, with faculties granted by the Military Ordinariate to exercise his priestly ministry in Camp Pendleton, Camp Del Mar, and Camp Stuart Mesa, California.

March 31, 1965:   Father Capodanno receives faculties and "personal parochial jurisdiction" over the 3rd Marine Division and all subjects of the Military Vicar in Okinawa and Vietnam.

April 6, 1966:   Assigned to depart via Okinawa for Vietnam, and granted faculties and "personal parochial jurisdiction" by the Military Ordinariate to exercise his priestly ministry to "All subjects of the Military Vicar assigned to or residing in Okinawa—also in Vietnam." Temporarily assigned to Chu Lai, Vietnam in the Danang Enclave.

May 10-15, 1966:   Battle: Operation Montgomery/Lien Kat 40 in Quang Ngai Province, Vietnam.

May 25-28, 1966:   Battle: Operation Mobile in Quang Ngai Province, Vietnam.

July 26-28, 1966:	Battle: Operation Franklin/ Operation Lien Kat 50 in Quang Ngai Province, Vietnam.
September 8-16, 1966:	Battle: Operation Fresno in Quang Ngai Province, Vietnam.
September 16-27, 1966:	Battle: Operation Golden Fleece in the Mo Duc District.
October 17, 1966:	Father Capodanno was awarded the Vietnamese Cross of Gallantry with Silver Star by the Republic of Vietnam for his bravery in exercising his priestly ministry during Operation Fresno.
November 20-27, 1966:	Battle: Operation Rio Blanco/Lien Ket 70 in the Quang Ngai Province, Vietnam.
December 9, 1966:	Father Capodanno transferred to the 1st Medical Battalion as Catholic chaplain at the Marine hospital in Chu Lai.
January 4, 1967:	Father Capodanno submitted to the Navy his request for an extension of overseas duty.
January 26, 1967:	Operation DeSoto in the Quang Ngai Province, Vietnam.
May 4, 1967:	Father Capodanno was awarded the Vietnamese Cross of Gallantry with Bronze Star by the Republic of Vietnam for "meritorious services rendered during Operation Fresno and Golden Fleece."
May 11, 1967:	Father Capodanno was awarded the National Defense Medal and the

	Vietnamese Defense Medal with Fleet Marine Force Combat Operations Insignia and a 3/16-inch bronze star.
May 26, 1967:	Father Capodanno was awarded the Bronze Star by the President of the United States for his role with the United States Marines during the period May 1-December 9, 1966: Operations Mobile, Franklin, Fresno, Golden Fleece, and Rio Blanco.
June 10, 1967:	Assigned to 1st Battalion, 5th Marines at Tam Ky as Catholic chaplain, and, three weeks later, to the 1st Battalion, 7th Marines. Father Capodanno voluntarily begins night patrols with the Marines. He is the first chaplain to "walk the lines" to be with the Marines exposed to hostile night attacks.
July 10, 1967:	Father Capodanno submitted to the Navy his request for a six month extension of his overseas tour of duty in Vietnam, requesting to remain with the 1st Marine Division.
August 2, 1967:	Request for extension of overseas duty denied. Father Capodanno was needed in Newport, Rhode Island to train new chaplains.
August 15, 1967:	Assigned to the 3rd Battalion, 5th Marines.
August 27, 1967:	Father Capodanno repeated his request for extended tours of duty in Vietnam. All requests were denied.

September 4, 1967:   Battle: Operation Swift in the Que
                          Son Valley, Vietnam. While
                          ministering to wounded and dying
                          Marines on the battlefield, Father
                          Capodanno was killed shielding a
                          wounded Marine from sniper fire.

                          *****

May 19, 2006:   Public decree issued declaring
                          Father Capodanno as **Servant of
                          God**, as the Cause for Beatification
                          and Canonization is opened.

Priesthood ordination, 1958.

Bibliography

Books

Adams, David E. *Hill-55, Just South of Danang, Vietnam.* Bloomington, IN: 1st Books Library, 2002.

Glass, Doyle D. *Swift Sword. The Marines of Mike 3/5.* Louisville, KY: Coleche Press, 2014.

Miller, Ed Mack. *Maryknoll—At Work in the World.* Peekskill, NY: Maryknoll Fathers, 1974.

Mode, Daniel L. *The Grunt Padre. Father Vincent Robert Capodanno, Vietnam 1966-1967.* Oak Lawn, IL: CMJ Marian Publishers, 2000.

Murphy, Edward F. *Semper Fi Vietnam: From Danang to the DMZ Marine Corps Campaigns, 1965-1975.* New York, NY: Ballantine Books, 1997.

Plus, Raoul. *Radiating Christ.* Oak Lawn, IL: CMJ Associates, 1998.

Powers, George C. *The Maryknoll Movement.* Maryknoll, NY: Maryknoll Catholic Missionary Society, 1926

Schulzinger, Robert D. *A Time for War: The United States and Vietnam, 1941-1975.* New York, NY: Oxford University Press, 1997.

Turley, G.H. *The Easter Offensive, Vietnam, 1972.* New York, NY: Warner Books, 1989.

West, F.J., Jr. *The Village.* New York, NY: Bantam Books, 1992.

Periodicals

"Editorial on Cardinal Mindszenty; Words of Msgr. Sheen." *China Missionary*, vol. ii, no. 4 (April, 1949), pp. 429-430.

"Consecration of First Native Born Chinese Bishop." *China Missionary Bulletin*, vol. ii (iii), no.1 (January, 1950), p. 95.

"Imprisonment of Bishops Walsh and Kung seen as Proof of Continued Resistance to Communism by Catholics in Red China." *Asia*, vol. xii, no. 5 (May, 1960), pp. 532-534.

"Red China's Sentencing of Bishops Walsh and Kung Lauded by Schismatic Groups." *Asia*, vol. xii, no. 6 (June, 1960), p. 648.

"Bishops' Relief Agency Aids Thousands Made Homeless by Devastating Flood in Taiwan." *Mission Bulletin*, vol. xi, no. 8 (November 1959), pp. 987-988.

"'Bright Spot in Taiwan Floods, Was Co-operation of all,' Says Taiwan Missioner." *Mission Bulletin*, vol. xi, no. 9 (December 1959), pp. 992-1093.

"Chaplain, Ex-Taiwan Missionary Feels His Job is with Viet Troops." *The American Weekend*, October 19, 1966, p. 5.

"Padre is 7th Regiment Marines' Morale Booster on Cong Hunt." Kenneth Armstrong, *Cleveland Plain Dealer*, September 4, 1965, pp. 3-4.

Made in the USA
Middletown, DE
12 September 2018